Rome

Berlitz Publishing Company, Inc.
Princeton Mexico City London Eschborn Singapore

Berlitz Trademark Reg. U.S. Patent Office and other countries
Marca Registrada

Text:	Patricia Schultz
Editor:	Alice Fellows
Photography:	Chris Coe except pages 75 (Kay Reese), 62 (Tina Lee), and 78 (Daniel Vittet)
Cover Photo:	Chris Coe
Photo Editor:	Naomi Zinn
Layout:	Media Content Marketing, Inc.
Cartography:	Rafaelle De Gennaro

The author would like to acknowledge the kind hospitality extended
to her by British Airways.

*Although the publisher tries to insure the accuracy of all the infor-
mation in this book, changes are inevitable and errors may result.
The publisher cannot be responsible for any resulting loss, incon-
venience, or injury. If you find an error in this guide, please let the
editors know by writing to Berlitz Publishing Company, 400
Alexander Park, Princeton, NJ 08540-6306.*

ISBN 2-8315-7705-5

Printed in Italy

030/107 RP

CONTENTS

• A (☛) in the text denotes a highly recommended sight

Rome

ROME AND THE ROMANS

For the Jubilee of 2000, the Italian and Roman city governments wanted to put the best face possible on the Eternal City to welcome the millions of pilgrims expected from all over the world. Billions of lire were spent (3,000 billion to be exact) on *Roma Capitale*, a massive program of public works designed to enhance the status of the city and restore many artistic monuments, churches, archeological sites, and museums. More than 20 billion lire each were spent on the Roman Forum and the Villa Giulia (the Etruscan museum), and almost 2 billion for the church of San Pietro in Vincoli, to give but a few examples.

Many projects have been completed; for countless others the work continues. Public transportation is much improved, with a fleet of mostly new buses. Campo dei Fiori has been completely repaved with the famous *san pietrini*, the cobblestones unique to Rome. Museum hours have been extended, and at least one major exhibit on an international level is always to be found. The main railway station, *Stazione Termini,* has not only had a complete facelift, but was given a new life, with improved illumination; a supermarket, shops, and boutiques on the lower level; new ticket counters; and other much needed amenities.

The ancient Romans rushed out to conquer an empire and to make their city the *caput mundi* — "capital of the world." Except for this recent flurry of activity, their descendants have not been quite as ambitious in this field. Since Rome became the capital of the newly united Italy in 1870, the nation's seat of government has had a record somewhat marked by inefficiency and inertia. Despite the pressures of modern life, the hurtling traffic, and bustling activity in markets and on the streets, the pace of life in Rome is still rather provincial and leisurely. Geographically as well as psycho-logically, the city is closer to the laid-back south than to the can-do north of Italy.

In the 27 centuries of its existence, Rome has seen empires rise and fall, popes and caesars come and go, and artistic movements flourish and fade. Throughout all the different eras, however, there has been one strong thread of continuity: the Eternal City has always been changing.

Rome certainly doesn't stand still today. As a modern European capital, it can't afford to rest on its laurels. Rome must play the part of an up-to-date political and business city while simultaneously attempting to preserve its unparalleled cultural inheritance.

The wealth of Rome's patrimony makes most other cities look like paupers. For a start, there are its great ancient remains: the Pantheon, still awe-inspiring after almost 2,000 years; the imposing majesty of the Colosseum; the poignant ruins of the Roman Forum. Then there is the cool beauty of the early Christian basilicas and the heritage of medieval Rome, complete with all its glorious mosaics and tranquil cloisters. The Renaissance is reflected in elegant churches, graceful palaces, and the renowned genius of artists Raphael and Michelangelo. Finally, as if that wasn't enough, the Baroque era offers dynamic architecture, theatrical piazzas, and flamboyant fountains.

Visitors will quite likely be bowled over by this uncontested panoply of treasures, but today's Romans take them in their stride. They're accustomed to conducting their lives against this awesome backdrop, drinking tap water from an aqueduct most likely constructed by a Roman consul and restored by a Renaissance pope.

Perhaps Romans take Rome too much for granted. While it's refreshing that the city is not treated as an open-air museum, it's also true that many museums and other treasures remain closed for years on end while bureaucrats and politicians wrangle over renovation costs and funds wind up in the wrong pockets. Medieval Romans burned marble statues to obtain lime; modern Romans' love affair with the internal-combustion engine does almost as much damage. During the last few decades, exhaust fumes and traffic vibrations have had a catastrophic impact on monuments. So much of the grime has been removed for the Jubilee; so much still remains.

Rome is celebrated as having one of the richest and longest histories in the world.

Things are improving, however. Most traffic has been banned from large areas of the historic center, church façades have been given face-cleanings, and decades-old scaffolding has been removed from ancient columns and triumphal arches. The magnificent equestrian bronze statue of Emperor Marcus Aurelius, which spent most of the 1980s undergoing restoration, is now firmly back on the Campidoglio — albeit behind protective glass inside the Capitoline museums while a reproduction has taken its place outside in the center of the piazza.

Visitors should not fret over whether or not to follow the famous maxim of "when in Rome...." The rhythms of the Roman day will oblige you to do as the Romans do. For instance, you'll soon discover that there's no point in trying to toil round the

St. Peter's Square has long been ground zero for tourists and religious pilgrims alike.

sights in the afternoon heat, since most of the museums and churches will not be open anyway. Rather, this is the time to join the local ways. Seek out the shade of palms and pines in one of Rome's parks, or else soak up the atmosphere in a stage-set piazza, admiring the play of sunlight on weathered russet and ochre facades, listening to the water music of the continually splashing Baroque fountains, and enjoying one of the refreshing drinks the Romans do so well: perhaps a cool *spremuta d'arancio* made from freshly squeezed blood oranges, or a creamy *frullato* fruit shake.

The streets begin to thin out after 8pm, and this is your cue to find somewhere to go and eat — and how well you'll eat! Remember that the finest Roman cuisine is based on the cooking of the poor; so your most memorable meal will most likely be found in a cozy restaurant in the old Jewish ghetto or a traditional *trattoria* in the working-class district of Trastevere, rather than in a smart establishment with a toney address.

Don't feel you have to plan every step in advance. Instead, copy the young English aristocrat who came to Rome on his Grand Tour in 1780 and decided to "straggle and wander about just as the spirit chooses."

A BRIEF HISTORY

Cherished legend claims that Rome was founded by Romulus, sired with twin brother Remus by Mars of a vestal virgin, and abandoned on the Palatine Hill to be suckled by a she-wolf. Historians agree that the site and traditional founding date of 753 B.C. are just about right.

Archeologists have further established that the site was occupied as early as the Bronze Age (c. 1500 B.C.). By the eighth century B.C. villages had sprung up on the Palatine and Aventine hills, and soon after on the Esquiline and Quirinal ridges. All these spots proved favorable for new settlements, since they were easily defensible and lay close to the midstream Isola Tiberina, which facilitated fording the river. After conquering their Sabine neighbors, the Romans merged the group of villages into a single city and surrounded it with a defensive wall. The marshland below the Capitoline Hill was drained and became the Forum. Under the consecutive rule of seven kings, Rome began to develop as a powerful force in central Italy.

The Roman Republic

A revolt by Roman nobles in 510 B.C. overthrew the last Etruscan king and established a Republic which was to last for the next five centuries. At first the young Republic, under the leadership of two patrician consuls, was plagued by confrontations between patrician and plebeian factions. The plebes then put forward their own leaders, the tribunes, to protect their interests. With a solid political order at home, Rome began to expand its influence.

In 390 B.C., the Gauls besieged the city for seven long months, destroying everything but the citadel on the Capitoline Hill. When the Gauls left, the hardy citizens set about reconstructing, this time enclosing their city in a wall of huge tufa blocks. For over eight centuries, until the Barbarians came, no foreign invader was to breach those walls.

Rome now spread its control to all of Italy, consolidating its hold with six military roads fanning out from the city — Appia, Latina, Salaria, Flaminia, Aurelia, and Cassia. By 250 B.C. the city's population had grown to an impressive 100,000.

Victory over Carthage in the Punic wars (264–146 B.C.) and conquests in Macedonia, Asia Minor, Spain, and southern France extended Roman power in the Mediterranean. When Hannibal crossed the Alps and invaded Italy in the Second Punic War, large areas of the peninsula were devastated and peasants sought refuge in Rome, swelling the population still further.

The acquisition of largely unsought territories brought new social and economic problems to the Roman people. Unemployment, poor housing, and an inadequate public works program provoked unrest within the city. Violent civil wars shook the Republic, which ultimately yielded to dictatorship. Former proconsul Julius Caesar, who had achieved some fame by subduing Gaul and Britain, crossed the tiny Rubicon River, which marked the boundary of his province, and marched boldly on Rome to seize power.

The Empire

Caesar's reforms, which bypassed the Senate, sought to combat unemployment, ease the tax burden, and make other reforms and made dangerous enemies. His assassination on the Ides of March in 44 B.C. led to a bitter civil war and to the despotic rule of his adopted son Octavian, who, as Augustus, became the first emperor. Under Augustus, the *Pax Romana* reigned supreme over the far-flung empire. To make Rome a worthy capital, he added fine public buildings

These intricate details found on the Arch of Constantine may have been taken from a monument to Marcus Aurelius.

in the form of baths, theaters, and temples, claiming he had "found Rome brick and left it marble." He also introduced public services, including the first fire brigade. This was the Golden Age of Roman letters, distinguished by poets and historians: Horace, Ovid, Livy, and Virgil.

In the first centuries of the empire, tens of thousands of foreigners flooded into Rome, among them the first Christians, including St. Peter and St. Paul. As this "new religion" gained ground, the emperors tried to suppress it, but the steadfastness of its adherents and their willingness to become martyrs only increased its appeal.

Each of Augustus's successors contributed his own embellishments to Rome. After a disastrous fire ravaged the city in A.D. 64, Nero rebuilt it and provided himself with an ostentatious villa, the Domus Aurea (Golden House of Nero), on the Esquiline Hill. Hadrian reconstructed the Pantheon, raised a monumental mausoleum for himself (Castel Sant' Angelo), and retired to his magnificent estate, Villa Adriana at Tivoli.

In the late first and second centuries A.D. Rome reached its peak of grandeur, with a population over one million. Inherent flaws in the imperial system, however, began to weaken the power of the emperors and led eventually to the total downfall of the empire.

After the death of Septimius Severus in A.D. 211, 25 emperors — all made and unmade by the army — reigned in the short space of 74 years. Assassination often ended their reigns. Fire and plague took their toll on the city's population. In A.D. 283 the Forum was almost completely destroyed by fire, never to recover its former magnificence.

After a vision of the Cross appeared to him on a battlefield, the story goes, Emperor Constantine I converted to Christianity. He ensured that Christianity was tolerated by an edict passed in A.D. 313, and he built the first churches and basilicas in Rome. But in A.D. 331 he effectively split the empire in two when he moved the imperial seat to Byzantium (Constantinople). Many of the wealthy as well as talented artists joined him, a hemorrhage from which the old capital never recovered.

The Middle Ages

As the Western Empire went into decline, the Romans recruited Barbarians into the legions to help defend it against other outsiders. But the hired defenders soon joined the attackers, and the disenchanted and weary Roman populace failed to summon up the same enthusiasm to defend the city that they had shown in conquering an empire.

Wave after wave of dreaded Barbarians came to sack, rape, murder, and pillage: Alaric the Visigoth in 410, Attila the Hun, the Vandals, and the Ostrogoths. Finally the Barbarian chief Odoacer forced the last Roman emperor, Romulus Augustulus, to abdicate in 476. The Western Empire was at an end, although the Eastern Empire continued to prosper until 1453.

In the sixth century, Justinian re-annexed Italy to the Byzantine Empire and codified Roman law as the state's legal system. But, as later Byzantine emperors lost interest in Rome, a new power arose out of the chaos: the Papacy. Pope Leo I (440–461) asserted the Bishop of Rome as Primate of the Western Church, tracing the succession back to St. Peter. Pope Gregory the Great (590–604) showed statesmanship in warding off the Lombards, a Germanic tribe already established in the north of Italy. In the eighth century, citing a document, the *Donation of Constantine* (later found to be a forgery), the popes began to claim political authority over all of Italy.

Rome by this time had been reduced to a village, and its small population deserted the city when Barbarian invaders cut the imperial aqueducts. Seeking the powerful support of the Franks, Pope Leo III crowned their king, Charlemagne emperor in St. Peter's Basilica on Christmas Day 800. But the Pope in turn had to kneel in allegiance to the emperor, and this exchange of spiritual blessing for military protection sowed the seeds of future conflict between the papacy and secular rulers.

Over the next 400 years, Italy saw invasions by Saracens and Magyars, Saxons and Normans (who sacked Rome in 1084), with papal Rome struggling along as only one of many feudal city-states on the now tormented peninsula. The papacy, and with it Rome, was controlled by various powerful families from the landed nobility. As the situation in Rome degenerated into chaos — deplored by Dante in his

Divine Comedy — the popes fled in 1309 to comfortable exile in Avignon, and remained under the protection of the French king until 1377. Rome was left to the brutal rule of the Orsini and Colonna families.

The Renaissance

The popes, reestablished in Rome in 1377, harshly put down any resistance to their rule and remained dominant in the city for the next 400 years. During the 15th and 16th centuries, the papacy became a notable patron of the Renaissance, that remarkable effusion of art and intellectual endeavor which gloriously transformed medieval Rome from a squalid, crumbling, and fever-ridden backwater to one of the foremost cities of the Christian world.

It was Giorgio Vasari, facile artist and first-rate chronicler of this cultural explosion, who dubbed this movement a

rinascita, or rebirth of the glories of Italy's Greco-Roman past. The father of Rome's High Renaissance, Pope Julius II (1503–1513), was responsible for the new St. Peter's Basilica. He also commissioned Michelangelo to paint the ceiling of the Sistine Chapel and Raphael to decorate the Vatican's Stanze. Donato Bramante, the architect, got the nick-

Roof fresco of San Pietro in Vincoli, built on site where St. Peter was put on trial.

name *maestro ruinante* because of the countless ancient monuments he had dismantled for the Pope's megalomaniacal building plans. With the treasures uncovered during this process, Julius founded the Vatican's magnificent collection of ancient sculpture.

The exuberant life of Renaissance Rome was brutally snuffed out in May 1527, however, by the arrival of the German troops of Holy Roman Emperor Charles V. This was to be the last — and worst — sack of the city.

Counter-Reformation

Meanwhile the position of the papacy and the doctrines of the Church of Rome were being challenged by Luther, Calvin, and other leaders of the Protestant Reformation. The Counter-Reformation, formally proclaimed in 1563, reinforced the Holy Office's Inquisition to combat heresy and the Index to censor the arts. Italian Protestants fled and Jews in Rome were shut up in a ghetto. Art proved a major instrument of Counter-Reformation propaganda. As the Church regained ground, it replaced the pagan influences of classicism with a more triumphant image, epitomized by Bernini's grand Baroque altar canopy in St. Peter's. The Baroque would flourish in Rome as in no other Italian city.

In the 18th century, Spain's authority over many of Italy's states passed to the Hapsburgs of Austria, who were determined to curb papal power in Rome. The papacy lost prestige with the enforced dissolution of the Jesuits, suffered a crippling loss of revenue during Hapsburg church reforms, and finally sank to its lowest ebb.

In 1798 Napoleon's troops entered Rome, later seized the papal states, and proclaimed a Republic. They treated Pius VI with contempt and carried him off to be a virtual prisoner in France. His successor, Pius VII, was forced to proclaim

Napoleon as emperor and for his pains was also made prisoner, returning to Rome only after Napoleon was defeated in 1814.

During the French occupation, however, a national self-awareness began to develop among Italians to challenge the reestablishment of Hapsburg rule. Many people looked to Pope Pius IX to lead this nationalist movement, but he feared the spread of liberalism and held back. In 1848, when a Republic was set up in Rome by Giuseppe Mazzini in the name of Italian nationalism, the Pope fled. He returned only in the following year, after the Republic had been crushed by the French army.

National unity for Italy was finally achieved in 1860 through the shrewd diplomacy of Prime Minister Cavour; the heroics of a guerrilla general, Giuseppe Garibaldi; and the leadership of King Vittorio Emanuele of Piedmont. Rome was captured by the nationalists in 1870 and became capital of Italy in the following year. Pope Pius IX retreated to the Vatican, a "prisoner of the monarchy."

The Modern Era

In World War I Italy was on the winning side against Austria and Germany. But after the peace conference of 1919, general disarray on the political scene led to an economic crisis, with stagnant productivity, bank closures, and rising unemployment. Threatened by the Fascists' March on Rome in 1922, King Vittorio Emanuele III meekly invited their leader, Benito Mussolini (Il Duce), to form a government.

Once firmly established in power, Mussolini made peace with the Pope through the Lateran Treaty of 1929, which created a separate Vatican state and perpetuated Roman Catholicism as the national religion of Italy. In 1940 Mussolini plunged Italy into the Second World War on the German side. Rome was declared an open city to spare it from bombing, and was liberated in 1944 with its treasures intact.

The initial post-war period was a time of hardship, but the 1950s saw Rome enjoying the fruits of Italy's "economic miracle." Jet-setting celebrities made the city their playground, finding *la dolce vita* in the nightspots of the Via Veneto. Meanwhile, Rome's population was soaring, as poor immigrants from Italy's south flocked into the city in search of work. Speculative developers threw up suburbs of shoddy blocks of flats on the urban periphery.

The city weathered a storm of left- and right-wing political terrorism when the 1970s became Italy's *anni di piombo* ("years of lead"). The darkest hour came in

Pope John Paul II brought the Roman Catholic Church into the new millenium.

1978 when the Red Brigades kidnapped and murdered the president of the Christian Democratic Party and former prime minister, Aldo Moro.

Sadly enough, as Rome's ancient monuments were being scrubbed clean in anticipation of the Jubilee 2000, a series of corruption scandals (*tangenti*) revealed the dirty hands of the capital's politicians in the mid 1990s. The political dust has settled and, with the hope of stability to come in the new millennium, Romans get on with their daily lives, coping with the present, preparing for the changes of the 21st century, and preserving their unparalleled past.

Artists and Architects Galore

BERNINI, GIAN LORENZO (1598–1680). As painter, sculptor, and architect, he was the foremost exponent of the Baroque. Among his works are St. Peter's Square, the Fountain of the Four Rivers in Piazza Navona, Palazzo Barberini, Galleria Borghese, and S. Maria della Vittoria.

BORROMINI, FRANCESCO (1599–1667). Baroque architect, he was assistant to and later the great rival of Bernini. He designed Sant'Agnese in Agone and the Palazzo Barberini.

BRAMANTE, DONATO (1444–1514). An architect and painter from Urbino, he was the foremost architect of the High Renaissance. He created the Belvedere Courtyard in the Vatican Museums.

DI CAMBIO, ARNOLFO (c. 1245–1302). Gothic architect and sculptor from Tuscany, his major works are Bonifacio IV's monument and the ciborium in St. Paul's.

CANOVA, ANTONIO (1757–1822). He created the Neo-classical sculpture of Napoleon's sister Pauline in the Borghese Gallery.

CARAVAGGIO, MICHELANGELO MERISI DA (1571–1610). He revolutionized art in the early 17th century with his bold use of foreshortening and dramatic *chiaroscuro* and his earthy realism. His paintings are in Santa Maria del Popolo, San Luigi dei Francesi, Palazzo Barberini, S. Agostino, and the Galleria Borghese.

MADERNO, CARLO (1556–1629). Architect from northern Italy, he is responsible for the facade of St. Peter's and the papal palace at Castel Gandolfo.

MICHELANGELO BUONARROTI (1475–1564). Florentine sculptor, architect, and reluctant painter, he is one of the most influential masters in the history of art. Among his creations are the dome of St. Peter's Basilica, the Sistine Chapel ceiling, *Moses* in the Church of St. Peter in Chains, and Campidoglio.

PINTURICCHIO, BERNARDINO (c. 1454–1513). This Tuscan-born artist painted frescoes in the Sistine Chapel, Borgia Apartments, and Santa Maria del Popolo.

RAPHAEL (RAFFAELLO SANZIO) (1483–1520). Painter and architect of the High Renaissance, among his works are the *Stanze* in the Vatican, the Chigi Chapel in Santa Maria del Popolo, and the painting *La Fornarina* in Palazzo Barberini.

WHERE TO GO

Visitors to Rome soon discover that cultural residues left behind from different eras are often interwoven: a pagan mausoleum is also a papal fortress, a medieval church has a Baroque facade, and a Renaissance palace overlooks a modern traffic junction. It doesn't matter whether you've come to Rome for the grandeur of the ancient remains, the revered pilgrimage sites of the Catholic Church, or the inspired works of Michelangelo, Raphael, and Bernini — you'll end up seeing a glorious hodge-podge of them all.

Although the municipality of Rome sprawls over a huge area, the principal sights are packed into a comparatively small zone. For the most part, the best way of getting about is on foot. Much of the historic center has been closed to traffic, and parking is generally impossible. Rome's public transport has been improved and although crowded during rush hours, it will usually get you near enough to your destination. We have grouped together the places which can be most conveniently visited on the same walking tour.

Before you make a special trip to a museum or monument, always check the hours with the Tourist Office (see page 123) or your hotel, or look in the local newspapers (see page 115).

THE CENTRO STORICO

The heart of Rome's historic center is the area that is enclosed by the bend of the River Tiber. Here, on what was once the exercise ground of Roman soldiers known as the Campus Martius or "Field of Mars," you will find vestiges of Rome's many different eras. Next to the remains of ancient temples there is a maze of medieval streets, as well as graceful Renaissance palazzi, ornate Baroque churches, sublime piazzas, and spectacular fountains. But the city center is up-to-date, too — among the monuments are contemporary shops, hotels, and the businesses of modern Rome.

Around Piazza Venezia

Piazza Venezia is the most convenient place to begin exploring. The hub of the capital's main traffic arteries, this is not really a place to linger, but is a principal stop on several major bus routes and in close proximity to a number of interesting sites.

As far as orientation is concerned, the massive **il Vittoriano** (Vittorio Emanuele Monument), is a landmark visible from all over the city. Romans wish the dazzling white marble, type-writer-shaped monument were not quite so conspicuous, and heap upon it such derisive nicknames as "Rome's False Teeth" and the "Wedding Cake." Built from 1885 to 1911 to celebrate the unification of Italy and dedicated to the new nation's first king, the Vittoriano contains the **Altare della Patria**, the tomb of Italy's Unknown Soldier of World War I, and has recently begun to host art exhibits.

> With people you know well, *ciao* is the casual form of greeting or farewell. *Salve* is a slightly less casual form.

A much more impressive work of architecture stands on the west side of the piazza: the **Palazzo Venezia**, the first great Renaissance palace in Rome. It was once the embassy of the Venetian Republic to the Holy See (hence its name), and in the 20th century served as Mussolini's official headquarters. His desk stood at the far corner of the Sala del Mappamondo, so positioned to intimidate visitors, who had to approach across the full 70-ft length of the marble floor. From the small balcony over the central door in the facade, *Il Duce* harangued his followers, amassed in the square below. The palace now contains a museum of medieval and Renaissance furniture, arms, tapestries, ceramics, and sculpture and occasionally hosts art exhibits.

The massive monument to Vittorio Emanuele also passes as the Tomb to the Unknown Soldier.

Capitoline Hill

Two flights of steps lead up behind the Vittorio Emanuele Monument. The more graceful and gradual, La Cordonata, takes you up between colossal statues of Castor and Pollux (mythical twin sons of Leda and the Swan), to the tranquil elegance of the **Piazza del Campidoglio**, on top of the Capitoline Hill, the smallest of Rome's seven hills.

This was once the Capitol, where the Temple of Jupiter Optimus Maximus Capitolinus stood, the most sacred site in ancient Rome. Today the Campidoglio is the site of a glorious Renaissance square, designed by Michelangelo (who also designed La Cordonata staircase), on the command of Pope Paul III, for the reception of the Holy Roman Emperor Charles V. Michelangelo also remodelled the existing **Palazzo Senatorio**, Rome's for-

Climb the steps to the top of Campidoglio and the elegantly designed piazza.

mer town hall, and planned the two palaces which flank it, the Palazzo dei Conservatori and the Palazzo Nuovo, although other architects completed them after his death.

As a centerpiece for the piazza, Michelangelo placed the magnificent bronze **statue of Marcus Aurelius** from the second century A.D. in the square. According to legend, it was so lifelike that Michelangelo commanded it to walk. The statue in the square is a copy; the original is displayed within the Palazzo Nuovo.

The **Capitoline Museums**, in the palaces of the Campidoglio, have extensive collections of magnificent sculpture excavated from ancient Rome. The **Palazzo Nuovo** (on the left) contains row upon row of portrait busts of Roman emperors (a good introduction to Classical Rome — see page 39), although its highlights are the poignant statue of the *Dying Gaul*, the sensual *Capitoline Venus*, a Roman copy of a Greek original dating from the second century B.C., and the *Marble Faun*, which gave its name to Hawthorne's romance. In the courtyard of the more visited **Palazzo dei Conservatori** (on the right) are a giant marble head, hand, and foot: fragments from a 40-ft high colossal statue of Emperor Constantine II. The palace is also home to the famous **Capitoline She-Wolf** depicted suckling the infants Romulus and Remus. This Etruscan bronze has become the symbol of Rome. In the top-floor **Pinacoteca Capitolina** (Capitoline Picture Gallery) are many fine works by Caravaggio, Bellini, Velázquez, Rubens, and Titian.

Alongside the Palazzo Senatorio a cobbled road opens out on to a terrace, giving you the first glimpse (and the best view) of the ruins of the Roman Forum below (see page 39), stretching from the Arch of Septimius Severus to the Arch of Titus, with the Colosseum beyond. The steeper flight of steps up the Campidoglio climbs to the austere church of **Santa Maria in Aracoeli**, on the site of the great temple of Juno Moneta. The 13th-century church was the home of the curious and much-revered Santo Bambino (the Baby Jesus), kept in a separate little chapel. Unfortunately the statue, believed to have had miraculous powers, was stolen in 1994. Today the manger lies empty.

The Corso

The mile-long main street of central Rome runs in a straight line from Piazza Venezia to Piazza del Popolo. Known in ancient times as the *Via Lata*, the Corso derives its modern name from the carnival races, or *corse*, that were first held here in the 15th century under the spectacle-loving Venetian, Pope Paul II. Of all the races, the most thrilling was the *Corsa dei Barberi*, in which riderless Barbary horses, sent into a frenzy by saddles spiked with nails, charged pell-mell along the narrow thoroughfare to be halted at last by a large white sheet hung across the street. Today the mostly pedestrian Corso is lined with palaces and churches, and crowded with cafes, shops, department stores and shoppers. To experience the Roman tradition of **la passeggiata** or pre-dinner stroll, this is *the* place to be.

In the **Piazza Colonna**, the **column of Marcus Aurelius**, decorated with spiraling reliefs of the emperor's military triumphs, rises in front of the Italian prime minister's offices in the Chigi Palace. The statue of the soldier-emperor, which originally stood on top of the column, was replaced in 1589 by a statue of St. Paul.

On the **Piazza Montecitorio** next door, which is dominated by an Egyptian obelisk dating from the sixth century B.C., stands the **Camera dei Deputati** (Chamber of Deputies), Italy's legislative lower house, designed by Bernini as a palace for the Ludovisi family.

Continue toward the banks of the River Tiber and turn right on the Via della Scrofa to find the **Ara Pacis Augustae**, a fascinating monument housed in a glass-sided building. When fragments of this "Altar of Peace," commissioned to celebrate Augustus's victorious campaigns in Gaul and Spain, first came to light in 1568, they were dispersed among several European museums. The pieces were returned to Rome when the building's reconstruction began in the 1930s. Along the friezes you can make out Augustus (Rome's first emperor), with his wife Livia and daughter Julia, his friend Agrippa, and a host of priests, nobles, and dignitaries. Alongside the altar, the great mound encircled by cypresses is the **Mausoleum of Augustus**, repository of the

At the Piazza del Popolo, you might want to rest beside this majestic fountain.

ashes of the caesars (except for Trajan) until Hadrian built his own mausoleum (now the Castel Sant'Angelo, see page 51) on the other side of the Tiber River.

At its northern end, the Corso culminates in the graceful oval shape of the **Piazza del Popolo**, a truly exemplary piece of open-air urban theater (finally freed of parked cars), designed in 1818 by Giuseppe Valadier, former architect to Napoleon. The central obelisk, the city's largest, dates back to the Egypt of Ramses II (13th century B.C.). It was brought to Rome by Augustus and erected in the Circus Maximus. Pope Sixtus V had it moved here in 1589.

The square takes its name from the Renaissance church of **Santa Maria del Popolo**, built at the northern gateway to the piazza on the site of Nero's tomb to exorcize his ghost, reputed to haunt the area. In its Baroque interior is a superb fresco of the *Nativity* by the Umbrian painter Pinturicchio in the first chapel on the right, and Raphael's Chigi Chapel, built as a mausoleum for the family of wealthy Sienese banker and brilliant patron of the arts, Agostino Chigi. This chapel houses two fine sculptures by Bernini: *Habakkuk* and *Daniel and the Lion*. In the Cerasi Chapel to the left of the altar are two powerful works by Caravaggio, the *Conversion of St. Paul* and *Crucifixion of St. Peter*, notable for the dramatic use of light and shade and the skillful foreshortening of the figures.

The piazza's arched 16th-century **Porta del Popolo** marks the gateway to ancient Rome at the end of the Via Flaminia, which led from Rimini on the Adriatic Coast. In later years, pilgrims arriving in Rome by the gate were greeted by the imposing twin Baroque churches of Santa Maria dei Miracoli and Santa Maria de Montesanto, guarding the northern entrance to the Corso. Two of Rome's best loved cafés, Rosati and Canova, face each other across the handsome expanse.

To the east above the piazza, and reached by a monumental complex of terraces, the 19th-century **Pincio** gardens offer a panoramic view of the piazza and the city, especially at sunset, when the rooftops are tinged with purple and gold. Also the work of Valadier, the statue-populated gardens occupy the site of the first-century B.C. villa of Lucullus, a provincial governor who returned enriched by the spoils of Asia and impressed his contemporaries by his extravagant lifestyle. The gardens stretch on into the leafy, less formal park of the **Villa Borghese**, once the estate of Cardinal Scipione Borghese, the nephew of Pope Paul V. The extensive 226-acre grounds (4 miles in perimeter) contain the recently renovated Galleria Borghese (see page 69), housed in the cardinal's former summer palace, and Italy's finest Etruscan art collection, housed in the **Villa Giulia** (see p. 71).

> An *edicola* is an outdoor kiosk that sells newspapers, post-cards and often tickets for public transportation.

Lined with pine trees and open-air cafés, the Pincio promenade takes you past the **Villa Medici**, built in 1564 and bought by Napoleon as a home for the French National Academy. Today the villa is host to young French artists visiting Rome on scholarships.

Around the Piazza di Spagna

Now the city's most sophisticated and high-priced shopping district, the area around the **Piazza di Spagna** has been attracting foreigners for centuries. Aristocratic travelers on the Grand Tour came here, as did many of the most celebrated artists of the Romantic era, among them Keats (see below), Byron, Balzac, Wagner, and Liszt.

The area continues to attract a cosmopolitan crowd. Well-heeled visitors come for the elegant and exclusive high-fashion boutiques along the Via Condotti and its grid of neighboring cobbled streets. Meanwhile, the more casually shod linger on the glorious **Scalinata della Trinità dei Monti** (the Spanish Steps, named after the nearby residence of the Spanish Ambassador to the Vatican), the city's most popular rendezvous for young Romans and foreigners alike. The steps ascend in three majestic tiers to the 16th-century French church of **Trinità dei Monti**, which, with twin belfries and a graceful Baroque facade, is one of Rome's most distinctive landmarks. Pink azaleas adorn the steps in spring, and

There is no shortage of steps in Rome, as shoppers at the Piazza di Spagna are aware.

in summer they become the catwalk for an open-air fashion show upon which top Italian designers present their newest "made-in-Italy" collections.

At the foot of the steps lies the **Fontana della Barcaccia** (Fountain of the Ugly Boat), a marble fountain in the shape of a sinking boat. The design, variously attributed to Pietro Bernini or his far more famous son, Gian Lorenzo Bernini, is an ingenious solution to the problem of low pressure in the Acqua Vergine, the aqueduct that supplies this fountain (as well as the Trevi Fountain) with water.

The poet John Keats died of consumption in 1821 at the age of 26 in a small room overlooking the steps. His house, 26

Piazza di Spagna, has since been preserved as the **Keats-Shelley Memorial** and museum. On the other side of the steps, at number 23, the quintessentially English **Babington's Tea Rooms** is a pleasant old-world bastion of Anglo-Saxon calm and gentility that has been serving tea and scones since the 1890s, when it was opened by a Miss Babington and her friend Miss Cargill.

An even more venerable establishment is found on nearby Via Condotti. **Caffè Greco** has been a favorite haunt of writers and artists for over two centuries, and the autographed portraits, busts, and statues decorating the café attest to its distinguished clientele, among them Casanova, Goethe, Baudelaire, Buffalo Bill, Gogol, and Hans Christian Andersen. The thick hot chocolate served in the winter by frock-coated waiters is a long-time tradition among stylish Roman shoppers and strollers.

Follow the Via del Corso (in the direction of the Vittorio Emmanuele Monument), and after you pass the Piazza Colonna

on your right, look for signs on your left to the Trevi Fountain. The **Fontana di Trevi** never fails to astonish. Nicola Salvi's Baroque extravaganza seems a giant stage set, out of all proportion to its tiny piazza. The 18th-century fountain is in fact a triumphal arch and palace facade (for the old Palazzo Poli)

The great god Neptune presides over the enormous Fontana di Trevi.

which frames mythic creatures in a riot of rocks, fountains and pools, all theatrically illuminated at night. The centerpiece is the massive figure of Neptune, who rides on a seashell drawn by two winged sea horses led by tritons. The rearing horse symbolizes the sea's turmoil, the calm steed its tranquillity. Marcello Mastroianni and Anita Ekberg frolicked memorably in the fountain's legendarily pure waters (carried three miles by an ancient Roman aqueduct) when they starred in Federico Fellini's film *La Dolce Vita* (*The Sweet Life*). The authorities frown on that sort of behavior today, but you must throw a coin, with your right hand over your left shoulder, to ensure a return to Rome (coins are collected regularly and donated to the Red Cross). Pull up a marble step and enjoy some of the Eternal City's best people-watching.

Between Piazza Barbarini (see below) and the Imperial Forum, and dominating the summit of the highest of the seven hills of ancient Rome, is the Baroque **Palazzo del Quirinale**. This was the summer palace of the popes until the unification of Italy in 1870, when it became home of the new king of Italy. Since 1947 it has been the official residence of the president of the Republic. In the center of the vast Piazza del Quirinale, magnificent **statues of Castor and Pollux** and their steeds, all Roman copies of Greek originals, stand beside an ancient obelisk. The piazza affords a splendid view over the whole city towards St. Peter's.

Lovers of the Baroque era will find much to delight them in this part of the city, which teems with masterpieces of sculpture and architecture by Bernini. Opposite the *manica lunga* or "long sleeve" of the Quirinal Palace you will find the small but perfectly formed church of **Sant'Andrea al Quirinale**, while in the nearby **Piazza Barberini** (at the corner of the Via Veneto) are two of the 17th-century master's celebrated fountains: the **Fontana del Tritone**, which takes center stage, especially after its 1998 restoration, and the **Fontana delle Api**, on its north side (dedicated to the public and their animals). Both fountains sport the bee symbol taken from the Barberini coat of arms of Pope Urban VIII, Bernini's patron. The busy genius also had a hand in the architecture of the stately **Palazzo Barberini** (1625–1633), which now houses part of the Galleria Nazionale d'Arte Antica (see page 72).

The Piazza Barberini serves as a base for the fabled Via Veneto, that heads north from here to the green park of the Villa Borghese. Home to embassies, deluxe hotels, and outdoor cafés, the Villa Borghese is now only faintly evocative of the days when Rome was the heady and hedonistic Hollywood of Europe.

☛ Around the Piazza Navona

The beautiful **Piazza Navona** has been a prime spot for recreation since the time of Emperor Domitian, who laid out an athletics arena, Circus Agonalis, on this site in A.D. 79, which established the future piazza's oval shape.

Jousting tournaments took place here in the Middle Ages, and from the 17th to the 19th century it was the scene of spectacular water pageants in summer, when the fountains overflowed until the piazza was flooded. As bands played, the aristocracy reenacted in mock the battles of their ancient ancestors, to the delight of thousands of onlookers. Today the piazza remains Rome's perfect stage set, and the public spectacle continues. Secure a front-row seat at any of the alfresco cafés and enjoy the show supplied by artists, performers, musicians, and caricaturists, and the local and foreign observers they attract.

The Baroque centerpiece is Bernini's **Fontana dei Fiumi** (Fountain of the Four Rivers), which incorporates an ancient

Stepping into the interior of the majestic Pantheon is like time travel back to the days of the Roman Empire.

obelisk into a monumental allegory symbolizing the great rivers of the four continents: the Americas (Río de la Plata), Europe (the Danube), Asia (the Ganges), and Africa (the Nile). Romans who delight in Bernini's scorn for his rivals suggest that the Nile god is covering his head rather than having to look at Borromini's church of Sant'Agnese in Agone, and that the river god of the Americas is poised to catch it in case it collapses. In truth, the fountain was completed some years before Borromini's splendid — and structurally impeccable — facade and dome.

The magnificent **Pantheon**, in the nearby Piazza della Rotonda, is the best-preserved monument of ancient Rome. This "Temple of All the Gods" was saved for posterity when it was converted into a church (and was therefore untouchable) in the seventh century. The original Pantheon, built on this site in 27 B.C. by Marcus Agrippa (the son-in-law of Augustus), was destroyed by fire. Emperor Hadrian then rebuilt it around A.D. 125, but modestly left his predecessor's name on the frieze above the portico, which is supported by 16 monolithic pink-and-grey granite columns. The bronze beams which once adorned the entrance were taken away by the Barberini Pope Urban VIII to make Bernini's *baldacchino* canopy for the high altar in St. Peter's. His action prompted the saying: "Quod non fecerunt barbari, fecerunt Barberini" ("What the Barbarians didn't do, the Barberini did").

The Pantheon's true greatness is only fully appreciated once you step inside and look up into the magnificent coffered **dome**. Over 43 m (141 ft.) in diameter (exactly equal to its height), it is even wider than the mighty cupola of St. Peter's. Held up without any sustaining columns or flying butresses, the dome represents an unparalleled feat of architectural engineering. On fine days a shaft of sunlight lights up the windowless vault through the circular hole (*oculus*) in the dome (it also lets in the rain). The gods and goddesses are long gone, replaced by the Renaissance tombs of Raphael (and his mistress) and the architect Baldassare Peruzzi, as well as the first king of Italy, Vittorio Emanuele II, and his son Umberto I.

Around the Campo dei Fiori

The site of public executions during the 17th century, the **Campo dei Fiori** is now a bustling fruit, vegetable, and flower market, one of Rome's liveliest and most authentic. A reminder of the square's bloody past, however, is provided by the brooding statue of philosopher Giordano Bruno, who was burned alive here by the Counter-Reformation papacy in 1600.

Across the Corso Vittorio Emanuele, the great architects of the age worked on the **Palazzo Farnese**, Rome's finest

Fresh flowers adorn the Campo dei Fiori,
Rome's largest and most colorful open-air market.

Renaissance palace, whose facade has just recently been restored. Begun in 1514 by Antonio da Sangallo the Younger for Cardinal Alessandro Farnese (Pope Paul III), the project was passed on to Michelangelo, who was responsible for the top floor, and was finally completed in 1589 by Giacomo della Porta. The building cost so much that it put a great strain on the fortune Farnese had amassed while he was treasurer of the Church. Since 1871 the palace has been home to the French Embassy. You need special permission to see the ceremonial dining room's mythological frescoes by Annibale Carracci. Facing Palazzo Farnese, on the left of the square, is Palazzo Spada, a beautiful example of Renaissance art which houses a museum and art gallery.

Retrace your steps to the Campo dei Fiori. The narrow streets heading southeast of the marketplace take you into the

The remaining columns of the Teatro di Marcello commissioned by Julius Ceasar.

former **Jewish Ghetto**, a lively and historic district peppered with restaurants serving the city's distinctive Roman/Jewish cuisine. Jews were forced into this confined space in 1555 by Pope Paul IV. Rules were relaxed considerably after his death, but the walls that confined the quarter were not torn down until 1848. A small but vibrant Jewish community still lives in and around the Via del Portico d'Ottavia. The main synagogue, built in 1904 in the Assyrian-Babylonian style, sits down by the river bank, and houses a small museum of local Jewish history.

One of the most charming fountains in Rome and much loved by its children, is the 16th-century **Fontana delle Tartarughe** (Turtle Fountain), in Piazza Mattei. It depicts four boys perched on squirting dolphins while lifting four turtles onto an upper marble basin with gracefully outstretched arms.

Nearby is the **Portico d'Ottavia**, a crumbling arched facade more than 2,000 years old and dedicated to Augustus's sister. Beyond it extends the **Teatro di Marcello** (Theater of Marcellus), begun by Julius Caesar and finished under Augustus; it is said to have been the architectural model for the Colosseum.

The Ponte Fabricio, one of the Rome's oldest bridges (62 B.C.), links the left bank to the tiny **Isola Tiberina** (Tiber Island). Three centuries before Christ the island was the sacred property of Aesculapius, god of healing, to whom a temple and hospital were dedicated. A large hospital founded in 1548 stands here to this day, occupying most of the island and tended by the founding monks, the Brothers of St. John of God. A second bridge, Ponte Cestio, remodeled in the 19th century, leads over to the river's right bank and the neighborhood of Trastevere (see page 38).

The Aventine

Once revered as the "Sacred Mount" in ancient times, when it stood outside Rome's walls, the Aventine remains a quiet sanctuary above the clamor of the city. An aristocratic district in the Imperial era, the hill is still a favored residential zone, with villas and apartments set in shady gardens of flowers and palms.

The Aventine is also the site of some of the earliest Christian churches, the most beautiful of which is the basilica of **Santa Sabina** built around A.D. 425. The 24 white Corinthian columns lining the nave give the church a classic harmony, while the beautiful carved fifth-century cypress wood doors in the portico contain one of the earliest depictions of the crucifixion in Christian art. Through a window in the atrium you can see a descendant of an orange tree planted by St. Dominic in 1220. A few steps away stands the villa of the **Cavalieri di Malta** (Knights of Malta). Take a peep through the keyhole of the perpetually closed massive garden gates for an unusual view of the perfectly framed dome of St. Peter's in the distance, a favorite post-card subject.

At the foot of the Aventine near the Tiber, the little church of **Santa Maria in Cosmedìn** was given by the Pope to

Rome's Greek colony in the eighth century. Its Romanesque facade and simple interior, with beautiful polychrome floor mosaics, provide a stark contrast to the city's dominant Baroque grandeur. Test your honesty in the portico's fierce-looking **Bocca della Verità** (Mouth of Truth), made famous by Audrey Hepburn in the classic film *Roman Holiday*, on the left-hand wall of the portico. The 12th-century marble face is said to bite off the fingers of anyone putting a hand in the gaping mouth who tells a lie. So far, no hands have been lost.

Across the road, two of the city's most charming and best-preserved temples stand on what was once part of the ancient cattle market. The one with 20 fluted Corinthian columns is erroneously known as the **Temple of Vesta** — probably dedicated to Hercules — and is the oldest standing marble temple in Rome. Its rectangular neighbor, the **Temple of Virile Fortune**, is a victim of the classical scholar's equivalent of a typing error, as its presiding deity is believed to have been Portunus, god of harbors, rather than Fortuna.

South of the Aventine near Porta San Paolo, dark cypresses shade the beautiful **Protestant Cemetery**, where Keats is buried (d. 1821; see pages 29-30) and where the ashes of his friend Shelley are interred (d. 1822). Towering over the cemetery is Rome's only **pyramid**, having survived two millennia because of its incorporation into the city walls. A Roman colonial magistrate, Caius Cestius, commissioned the 100-ft-high monument for his tomb in 20 B.C. on his return from Egypt.

Trastevere

Trastevere, "Tevere across the Tiber," has been Rome's traditional working-class quarter since ancient times, and its inhabitants pride themselves on being the true Romans, a breed apart from the rest of the city. The word *Noiantri*, dialect for "we others," reflects the way they see themselves, and is also the name for their riverside festival of music, eating, and fireworks the last two weeks in July.

Despite recent gentrification that has dotted the district with smart shops, tearooms, clubs, and restaurants, Trastevere still displays its lively atmosphere and idiosyncratic character, particularly in the narrow cobbled streets around the Piazza di Santa Maria, the heart of the quarter. The church of **Santa Maria in Trastevere** is reputedly the oldest in the city. Its foundation (on the spot where oil is said to have gushed the day Jesus was born in Bethlehem) can be traced back to the third century A.D., but the present structure dates from 1130–1143 and is the work of Pope Innocent II, himself a Trasteverino. The facade is decorated with a beautiful and mysterious 13th-century mosaic of the Virgin flanked by ten maidens bearing lamps. Inside, the 12th-century Byzantine mosaics covering the floor and apse are its highlight.

Before entering the church of **Santa Cecilia in Trastevere**, pause in the courtyard to admire the russet Baroque facade and endearingly leaning Romanesque tower (1113 A.D.). Now regarded as the patron saint of music, St. Cecilia was martyred for her Christian faith in A.D. 230. Her chapel stands over the site of her home and the *caldarium* (the bathhouse, still visible) in which she was tortured by scalding; she was finally beheaded when these attempts didn't work. The sculptor Stefano Maderno was on hand when her tomb was excavated in 1599 and his beautiful statue shows the miraculously conserved body served as his model.

CLASSICAL ROME

The nucleus of classical Rome is around the Colosseum (see page 47), with the Forum to the northwest and the Baths of Caracalla (see page 49) to the south. Don't try to decipher each fragment of broken stone — not even archeologists have succeeded. It's far better to soak up the romantic atmosphere while reflecting on the ruined majesty of this ancient civilization. Take care to avoid summer's midday sun in the shadeless Forum and finish your visit with a picnic and siesta on the Palatine.

☞ The Roman Forum

You can stand among the columns, porticoes, and arches of the *Foro Romano* and, with an exhilarating leap of the imagination, picture the hub of the great Imperial City, the first city in Europe to boast a population of one million people.

Surrounded by the Palatine, Capitoline, and Esquiline hills and drained by the Cloaca Maxima, an underground channel, the flat valley of the Forum developed as the civic, commercial, and religious center of the growing city. Under the emperors, it attained unprecedented splendor, with its white marble and

Tour the Forum ruins with a guide or venture out alone and let your imagination roam.

the golden roofs of temples, law courts, and market halls glittering in the sun. After the Barbarian invasions, the area was abandoned. Subsequently fire, earthquakes, floods, and the plunder of Renaissance architects reduced the area to a

> For the most dramatic sight of the Forum, view it at night from the terrace beside the Palazzo Senatorio above, when it is floodlit.

muddy cow pasture, until excavations in the 19th century once again brought many of the ancient edifices to light. Grass still grows between the cracked paving stones of the Via Sacra, poppies bloom among the piles of toppled marble, and tangles of red roses are entwined in the brick columns, softening the harshness of the ruins.

Portable sound-guides can be rented at the entrance (on the Via dei Fori Imperiali) where questionably authorized independent guides-for-hire linger, or you can find your own way around the Forum. But before you embark on this, a sensible move is to make yourself comfortable on a chunk of fallen marble in the midst of the ruins and orient yourself, with the help of a detailed map, so that you can trace the layout of the ruins and make sense of the apparent confusion.

Start your tour at the west end, just below the Campidoglio's Palazzo Senatorio (see page 23). Here you can see how the arches of the Roman record office (*Tabularium*) have been incorporated into the rear of the Renaissance palace. From here, look along the full length of the **Via Sacra** (Sacred Way), the route taken by victorious generals as they rode in triumphal procession to the foot of the Capitoline Hill, followed by the legions' standards, massed ranks of prisoners, and carts piled high with the spoils of conquest.

Then, to counterbalance this image of the Romans as ruthless military conquerors, turn to the brick-built rectangular **Curia**, home of the Roman Senate, in the northwest corner of the Forum. Here you can gaze through the bronze doors (copies of the originals which are now in the church of St. John Lateran; see page 64) at the "venerable great-grandmother of all parliaments," where the senators, robed in simple togas, argued the affairs of Republic and Empire. The tenets of Roman law, which underpins most European legal systems, were first debated in this modest chamber.

Believed to mark the site of the very first assembly hall of the Roman elders, the Curia was constructed in its present form by Diocletian in A.D. 303. Its plain brick facade was once faced with marble. The church that covered it was dismantled in 1937 to reveal an ancient floor set with geometrical patterns in red and green marble, as well as the tiers on either side where the Roman senators sat, and the brick base of the gold-

---

The First Capitol Hill

To the Romans, the Capitol was both citadel and sanctuary, the symbolic center of government, where the consuls took their oath and the Republic's coinage was minted. Its name, now applied to many governments across the world, originated when a human skull was unearthed during excavations for the Temple of Jupiter — this was interpreted as a sign that Rome would one day be head (*caput*) of the world.

When the Gauls sacked Rome in 390 B.C., the Capitol was saved by the timely cackling of the sanctuary's sacred geese, warning that attackers were scaling the rocks. Later, victorious caesars ended their triumphal processions here. They rode up from the Forum in chariots drawn by white steeds to pay homage at the magnificent gilded Temple of Jupiter, which dominated the southern tip of the Capitoline.

In the Middle Ages, the collapsed temples were pillaged and the hill was abandoned to goats until, in the 16th century, Pope Paul III commissioned Michelangelo to give the Campidoglio its new glory.

This sculpture of Romulus and Remus suckling from a she-wolf is the rather unusual symbol of the city.

en statue of Victory at the rear. The Curia shelters two bas-reliefs, outlining in marble the ancient buildings of the Forum.

In front of the Curia, a concrete shelter protects the underground site of the **Lapis Niger** (usually not on view), a black marble stone placed by Silla over the (presumed) grave of Romulus, the city's founder. Beside it is a stele engraved with the oldest Latin inscription ever found, dating back some six centuries B.C.; no one has completely deciphered it yet.

The triple **Arco de Settimio Severo** (Arch of Septimius Severo) dominates this end of the Forum. Its friezes depict the eastern military triumphs of the third-century emperor who later campaigned as far as Scotland. Nearby is the orators' platform, or **Rostra**. Its name comes from the iron prows (*rostra*), which once adorned it, taken from enemy ships at the Battle of Antium in 338 B.C.

Two points have special significance: the *Umbilicus Urbis Romae*, which marks the traditional epicenter of Rome, and the *Miliarium Aureum* (Golden Milestone), which recorded in gold letters the distances in miles from Rome to the cities of the farflung empire.

Public meetings and ceremonies took place in the social forum in front of the Rostra, kept bare save for samples of three plants considered sacred to Mediterranean prosperity: the vine, the olive, and the fig. Still prominent above this open space is the **Colonna di Foca** (Column of Phocas), built to honor the Byzantine emperor who presented the Pantheon to Pope Boniface IV.

Eight tall columns standing on a podium at the foot of the Capitol belong to the **Tempio di Saturno** (Temple of Saturn), one of the earliest temples in Rome. It doubled as both state treasury and center of the December debauchery known as the Saturnalia, the pagan precursor of Christmas.

Of the **Basilica Julia**, which was once busy law courts (it was named after Julius Caesar who commissioned it), only the paving and some of the arches and travertine pillars survive. Even less remains of the Basilica Aemilia, on the opposite side of the Via Sacra, destroyed by the Goths in A.D. 410.

Three slender columns, the podium, and a portion of the entablature denote the **Tempio dei Dioscuri** (Temple of Castor and Pollux), built 484 B.C. It was dedicated to the twin sons of Leda and the Swan, after they appeared on the battlefield at Lake Regillus to rally the Romans against the Latins and the Etruscans.

The altar of Julius Caesar is tucked away in a semicircular recess of the **Tempio di Cesare** (Temple of the Divine Julius). On 19 March in 44 B.C., the grieving crowds, following Caesar's funeral procession to his cremation in the Campus Martius, made an impromptu pyre of chairs and tables and burned his body in the Forum.

Pause for a pleasant idyll in the **Casa delle Vestali** (Hall of the Vestal Virgins), surrounded by graceful statues in the serene setting of a rose garden and old rectangular fountain basins, once more filled with water. In the circular white marble

Tempio di Vesta (the Temple of Vesta), the sacred flame perpetuating the Roman state was tended by six Vestal Virgins, who from childhood observed a 30-year vow of chastity under threat of being buried alive if they broke it. They were under the supervision of the high priest, the Pontifex Maximus (the popes have since appropriated this title), whose official residence was in the nearby Regia, of which only overgrown brick vestiges remain.

Heads up — the Hall of Vestal Virgins is lined with stone goddesses.

The imposing **Temple of Antoninus and Faustina**, farther along the Via Sacra, has survived because, like the Curia, it was converted into a church, acquiring a Baroque facade in 1602. In addition, few ancient buildings can match the massive proportions of the **Basilica of Constantine and Maxentius**, completed by Constantine. Three giant vaults still stand.

The Via Sacra culminates in the **Arch of Titus**, built to commemorate the capture of Jerusalem in A.D. 70. Restored by Giuseppe Valadier in 1821, it shows in magnificent carved relief the triumphal procession of Titus bearing the spoils of the city, among them the Temple of Jerusalem's altar, a seven-branched golden minora, and silver trumpets.

From this end of the Forum a slope leads up to the **Palatine Hill**, Rome's legendary birthplace and today its most romantic garden, dotted with toppled columns among the wild flowers and spiny acanthus shrubs. At the time of the ancient Republic, this was a desirable residential district for the wealthy and aristocratic, including Cicero and Crassus. Augustus began the Imperial trend and later emperors added and expanded, each trying to outdo the last in magnificence and luxury until the whole area was one immense palace (the very word takes its name from the hill). From the pavilions and terraces of the 16th-century botanical gardens laid out here by the Farnese family, there is an excellent view of the whole Forum. A small **museum** (follow the signs) reopened up here in 1998.

The so-called **House of Livia** is now believed to be that of her husband, Emperor Augustus, who here combined modesty with taste. Small, graceful rooms retain remnants of mosaic floors. Nearby, a circular Iron Age dwelling unearthed from the time of Rome's legendary beginnings is

known as **Casa di Romolo** (Romulus' Home).

A subterranean passageway linking the palaces, the **Cryptoporticus of Nero**, threads through the Palatine. In the dim light you can just make out stucco decorations on the ceilings and walls. The vast assemblage of ruins of the Domus Flavia include a basilica, throne room, banqueting hall, baths, porticoes,

Towering Trajan's Column shoots skyward beside a Classical church dome.

and a fountain in the form of a maze. Together with the Domus Augustana, the complex is known as the **Palace of Domitian**. From one side you can look down into the **Stadium of Domitian**, which was probably a venue for horse races.

The last emperor to build on the Palatine, Septimius Severus, carried the imperial palace right to the southeastern end of the hill, so that his **Domus Severiana** was the impressive first glimpse of the capital for new arrivals. It was dismantled and its vast expanses of marble used to build Renaissance Rome.

From this edge of the Palatine you have a splendid view down into the immense grassy stretch of the **Circus Maximus**, where crowds of up to 300,000 watched chariot races from tiers of marble seats.

The **Fori Imperiali** (Imperial Forums) were built as an adjunct to the Foro Romano in honor of Julius Caesar, Augustus, Trajan, Vespasian, and Nerva. The most interesting corner is the Markets of Trajan, reopened to the public in 1998, where you can once again wander some of the best preserved ancient Roman streets. Here was a kind of ancient shopping mall, made up of 150 shops and offices. Duck through a tunnel to visit the remarkable 30 m (100 ft) **Trajan's Column** (A.D. 113). Celebrating Trajan's campaigns against the Dacians in what is now Romania, the minutely detailed friezes spiraling round the column constitute a veritable textbook of Roman warfare, featuring embarkation on ships, the clash of armies, and the surrender of Barbarian chieftains — in all, utilizing some 2,500 figures. St. Peter's statue atop the column replaced the emperor's in 1587.

The Colosseum

It says something about the essential earthiness of Rome that, more than any inspirational church or palace, it is the

The Arch of Constantine and Colosseum are some of the most photographed sites in all of Rome.

Colosseum that is the very symbol of the city's eternity. Built in A.D. 72–80 by slaves and prisoners, the four-tiered elliptical amphitheater seated some 50,000 spectators on stone benches, according to social status.

The gladiators were originally criminals, war captives, and slaves; later, free men entered the "profession," tempted by wealth and fame. Contrary to popular belief, there is little historical evidence to support the image of the Colosseum as the place where Christians were fed to the lions. Audio guides for rent at the entrance help bring alive those raucous days. An elaborate restoration, completed in 1999, has extended the areas and hours now open to visitors.

Popes and princes stripped the Colosseum of its precious marble cladding, its travertine and metal for their churches and palaces. They have left behind a ruined maze of cells and corridors which funneled both men and beasts to the slaughter. The horror (Byron called the Colosseum "the gladiator's bloody circus") has disappeared beneath the moss, but the thrill of the monument's endurance remains. As an old Anglo-Saxon prophecy goes: "While stands the Colosseum, Rome shall stand; when falls the Colosseum, Rome shall fall; and when Rome falls, with it shall fall the world."

The nearby **Arch of Constantine** celebrates Constantine's victory over his imperial rival Maxentius at Saxa Rubra. He may have won the battle, but a cost-conscious Senate took fragments from monuments of earlier rulers Trajan, Hadrian, and Marcus Aurelius to decorate the arch.

Immediately northeast of the Colosseum is the **Domus Aurea**, the fabulous villa with extensive gardens built by the emperor Nero, who spent very few years in his "Golden House" before killing himself in A.D. 68. It was reopened to the public in 1999 after 15 years of renovation work. Although extremely interesting for students, archeologists, and art historians, other visitors may be disappointed, as there's very little left of the lavish mosaics, frescoes, inlaid floors, and paintings in gold. The last room on the obligatory tour (every half hour), the octagonal hall with its open skylight, is the most impressive. Renderings of the glory of the original 250-room villa (of which only 30 can be visited), built on a site that was 25 times the size of the Colosseum, would be an enormous help here.

Terme di Caracalla

The huge third-century Baths of Caracalla, 1 km (0.6 mile) south of the Colosseum, were built for people to bathe in considerable style and luxury. Public bathing was a prolonged social event. Senatoras and merchants passed from the *caldarium* (hot room) to cool down in the *tepidarium* and the *frigidarium*. The baths ran dry in the sixth century when Barbarians cut the aqueducts. Until 1994, the massive *caldarium* was the stage of spectacular open-air operas, at present banned to protect the site. Rumors live on that *Aida* will once again be performed here.

THE VATICAN

The power of Rome endures both in the spirituality evoked by every stone in St. Peter's Basilica and in the physical awe inspired by the splendors of Vatican City. At their best, the popes and cardinals replaced military conquest by moral leadership and persuasion; at their worst, they could show the same hunger for political power and wealth as any caesar or grand duke. A visit to the Vatican is an object lesson for faithful and skeptic alike.

Constantine, first Christian emperor, erected the original St. Peter's Basilica in 324 over an oratory on the presumed site of the Apostle's tomb in A.D. 67. After it was sacked in 846 by marauding Saracens, Pope Leo IV ordered massive walls to be built around the sacred church, and the enclosed area became known as the Leonine City, and later Vatican City, after the Etruscan name of its location.

The Vatican became the main residence of the popes only after 1378, when the papacy was returned to Rome from exile in Avignon (see page 65). It has been a sovereign state, independent of Italy, since the Lateran Pact signed with Mussolini in 1929. The Pope is supreme ruler of this tiny state, which is guarded by an elite corps of Swiss Guards, founded in 1506, who still wear the blue, scarlet, and orange uniforms said to have been designed by Michelangelo. The papal domain has its own newspaper, *L'Osservatore Romano*, and a radio station which broadcasts worldwide. It also has shops, banks, a minuscule railway station (rarely used), and a post office that will get your postcards home far more quickly than the Italian postal service.

Apart from the 1 square km (0.4 square mile) comprising St. Peter's Square, St. Peter's Basilica, and the papal palace and gardens, the Vatican also has jurisdiction over extraterritorial enclaves, including the basilicas of St. John Lateran, Santa Maria Maggiore, and St. Paul's, as well as the Pope's summer residence at Castel Gandolfo (see page 54).

You don't need a passport to cross the border, and in fact you hardly even notice that you have — though it is marked by a band of white travertine stones running from the ends of the two colonnades at the rim of St. Peter's Square. The **Vatican Tourist Information Office** on the south side of St. Peter's Square arranges guided tours and issues tickets to the grounds of Vatican City, including the gardens. From here buses leave regularly for the Vatican Museums, also reached by foot in 20 minutes from the piazza.

A visit to St. Peter's combines ideally with a tour of the Castel Sant'Angelo, but it's best to save the Vatican Museums for a separate day: their four miles of galleries are best savored in small doses.

Castel Sant'Angelo

Cross the Tiber by the **Ponte Sant'Angelo**, which incorporates arches of Hadrian's original bridge, the Pons Aelius, built in A.D. 134. Ten windswept angels designed and sculpted by Bernini and his studio between 1598–1660, each bearing a symbol of the Passion of Christ, adorn the balustrades. This is the most beautiful of the 20-some bridges that cross the Tiber.

From the bridge you have the best view of the cylindrical bulk of the **Castel Sant'Angelo**, its mighty brick walls stripped of their travertine and pitted by cannonballs, but nevertheless standing up well to the ravages of time. Conceived

*The marble angels line the Ponte Sant'Angelo
that leads up to the Castel Sant'Angelo.*

by Hadrian as his family mausoleum, it became part of the defensive Aurelian Wall a century later. The castle gained its present name in A.D. 590 after Pope Gregory the Great had a vision of the Archangel Michael alighting on a turret and sheathing his sword to signal the end of a plague. For centuries this was Rome's mightiest military bastion and a refuge for the popes in times of trouble; Clement VII holed up here during the sack of Rome by Hapsburg troops in 1527.

A spiral ramp, showing traces of the original black-and-white mosaic paving, leads up to the funerary chamber where the ashes of emperors were kept in urns. You emerge into the **Cortile dell'Angelo** (Courtyard of the Angel), which is stacked neatly with cannonballs and watched over by a marble angel. An arms museum opens off the courtyard.

After the grimness of the exterior, it comes as a surprise to step into the luxurious surroundings of the old **Papal**

Apartments. Lavish frescoes cover the walls and ceilings of rooms that are hung with masterpieces by Dosso Dossi, Nicolas Poussin, and Lorenzo Lotto. Off the Courtyard of Alexander VI is possibly the most exquisite bathroom in history. The tiny room, just wide enough for its marble bathtub, is painted with delicate designs over every inch of its walls and along the side of the bath.

A harsh jolt brings you back to reality as you enter the **dungeons**, scene of torture and executions. You have to bend over double to get into the bare, stone cells where famous prisoners languished — among them sculptor-goldsmith Benvenuto Cellini and philosopher and monk Giordano Bruno.

The **Gallery of Pius IV**, surrounding the entire building, affords a panoramic view, as does the terrace on the summit, with the 18th-century bronze *Statue of St. Michael* by Verschaffelt. Opera lovers will recall this as the setting for the final act of Puccini's *Tosca*, in which the heroine hurls herself to her death from the battlements.

St. Peter's

From the Castel Sant'Angelo a wide, straight avenue, the Via della Conciliazione, leads triumphantly up to St. Peter's. A maze of medieval streets, in which stood Raphael's studio, was destroyed in 1936 by Mussolini's architects to provide an unobstructed view of St. Peter's all the way from the banks of the Tiber. A thick wall running parallel to the avenue conceals a passageway (*Il Passetto*) linking the Vatican to the Castel Sant'Angelo, by which the fleeing popes could reach their bastion in safety.

In **Piazza San Pietro** (St. Peter's Square), his greatest creation, Bernini managed to conceive one of the world's most exciting pieces of architectural orchestration. The sweeping curves of the colonnades reach out to embrace Rome and the whole world, *urbi et orbi*, to draw the flood of pilgrims into the bosom of the church. On Easter Sunday as many as 300,000 people cram into the piazza. The square is on or near the site of Nero's Circus, where early Christians were martyred.

Bernini completed the 284 travertine columns and 88 pilasters topped by 140 statues of the saints in just 11 years, from 1656 to 1667. In the center of the ellipse rises a 25-m (82-ft.) red granite **obelisk**, brought here from Egypt by Caligula in A.D. 37. Stand on one of the two circular paving stones set between the obelisk and the twin 17th-century fountains to see the quadruple rows of perfectly aligned Doric columns appear magically as one.

By any standards a grandiose achievement, **St. Peter's Basilica** does inevitably suffer from the competing visions of all the master architects called in to collaborate — Bramante, Baldassare Peruzzi, Giuliano da Sangallo, Carlo Maderno, Giacomo della Porta, Raphael, Michelangelo, and

---

Seeing the Pope

When he's not in Bogotà or Cairo, it is possible to see the Pope in person at his personal residence, the Vatican. He normally holds a public audience every Wednesday at 10am in a large modern audience hall. An invitation to a papal audience may be obtained from the Pontifical Prefect's Office (open morning, Monday–Saturday; Tel. 06-69883273, fax 06-69885863) in St. Peter's Square. It's advisable to book at least one month in advance.

On Sundays at noon, the Pope appears at the window of his apartments in the Apostolic Palace (to the right of the basilica, overlooking the square), delivers a brief homily, says the Angelus, and blesses the crowd below. On a few major holy days, the pontiff celebrates high mass in St. Peter's and may make an appearance on the basilica's open balcony.

The spectacular colonnades in St. Peter's Square have beckoned to the people of Rome and beyond for over 300 years.

Domenico Fontana, each of whom added, subtracted, and modified, often with a pope peering over his shoulder.

From 1506, when the new basilica was begun under Julius II (replacing the original church built in the fourth century by Constantine), until 1626 when it was consecrated, St. Peter's Basilica was to change form several times. It started out as a simple Greek cross, with four arms of equal length, as favored by Bramante and Michelangelo, and ended up as Maderno's Latin cross, extended by a long nave, as demanded by the popes of the Counter-Reformation. One result is that Maderno's porticoed facade and nave obstruct a clear view of Michelangelo's dome from the square. Goethe once said that entering the basilica is "like entering eternity." The world's largest Roman Catholic church certainly has immense dimensions: 212 m (695 ft.) long on the outside, 187 m (613 ft.) inside, and 132 m (435 ft.) to the tip of the

Designed by Michelangelo, St. Peter's dome catches the light of the sunrise — it is a prominent element of the skyline.

dome. Brass markers on the floor of the central aisle show how far other famous cathedrals fail to measure up.

You'll find the basilica's most worthy artistic treasure, Michelangelo's sublime *Pietà* (1500), in its own chapel to the right of the entrance. The artist was only 25 when he executed this deeply moving marble sculpture of the Virgin cradling the crucified Christ in her lap. This is the only work which he bothered to sign (on the ribbon that crosses the Madonna's breast), after overhearing people crediting it to another sculptor. Since the statue was attacked by a religious fanatic with a hammer in 1972 (the tip of the Virgin's nose was broken off, but immediately restored), it has been protected by bulletproof glass. Reverence can also cause damage: On the 13th-century bronze *Statue of St. Peter* the toes of the right foot have been worn away by the lips and fingers of countless pilgrims.

Beneath the dome, Bernini's great *baldacchino* (canopy) soars over the high altar, at which only the Pope may celebrate mass. The canopy and four spiraling columns were cast from bronze beams taken from the Pantheon (see page 33). At the bottom of each column is a coat of arms bearing the three bees of the Barberini Pope Urban VIII, who commissioned the work. In the apse is an even more extravagant Baroque work, Bernini's bronze and marble *Cathedra of St. Peter*, throne of the Apostle's successors, into which the wooden chair of St. Peter is supposedly incorporated. Also by Bernini is the tomb of Pope Urban VIII, found here in the apse.

For his imposing **dome**, Michelangelo drew inspiration from the Pantheon and Brunelleschi's cupola on Florence's cathedral. A lift takes you as far as the gallery above the nave, from where there is a dizzying view down into the interior of the basilica, as well as close-ups of the inside of the dome. Spiral stairs and ramps lead on and up to the outdoor balcony which circles the top of the dome for stunning views of St. Peter's Square, Vatican City, and all of Rome.

The **Vatican Grottoes** beneath the basilica contain the tombs of popes and numerous little chapels. The **necropolis**, even deeper underground, shelters several pre-Christian tombs, as well as a simple monument which marks St. Peter's alleged burial place. This excavated area is not open to general viewing and visits should be arranged in advance through the Ufficio Scavi (Excavations Office, which you'll find just beyond the Arco della Campana to the left of the basilica).

Masses are said frequently in the side chapels, in various languages. St. Peter's has strict rules about modest dress: Visitors wearing shorts or other scanty attire are politely turned away.

The Vatican Museums

It should come as no surprise that the Roman Catholic Church, the world's greatest patron to painters, sculptors, and architects, should have in its headquarters one of the richest collections of art in the world. The 7 km (4 miles) of rooms and galleries of the **Vatican Museums** offer a microcosm of Western civilization. There is an almost bewildering profusion, from Egyptian mummies, Etruscan gold jewelry, and Greek and Roman sculpture, to medieval and Renaissance masterpieces to modern religious art. On a single ticket you can visit eight museums, five galleries, the Apostolic Library, Borgia Apartments, Raphael Rooms, and, of course, the incomparable Sistine Chapel.

Once past the entrance, and after an elevator ride to the starting point, choose between four color-coded itineraries which range from 1 hour (A, violet) to 5 hours (D, yellow).

With the booty from the ruthless dismantling of ancient monuments to make way for the Renaissance city in the 16th century, the **Museo Pio-Clementino** has assembled a wonderful collection of classical art. The most celebrated piece is the first century B.C. *Laocoön* group: the Trojan priest and his two sons who were strangled by serpents sent by the goddess Athena for refusing to allow the Greek horse to enter Troy.

Working Solo on the Ceiling

Painting the Sistine Chapel ceiling wasn't easy. Michelangelo, a sculptor of marble who had only a limited experience of oil painting, had never before produced a fresco — but this did not discourage Pope Julius II who commissioned the work. Preferring his own inexperience to their incompetence, the Florentine artist fired his seven assistants in the first couple of weeks and continued alone for four years, from 1508 to 1512. Contrary to legend, he did not lie on his back, but painted erect on tiptoe, bent backwards "like a Syrian bow." The Pope periodically climbed the scaffolding to check on his progress, threatening to throw him off his platform if he didn't hurry up. "I'm not in a good place," he wrote to a friend, "and I'm no painter."

Famous during Imperial times, it was unearthed from a vineyard on the Esquiline in 1506, to the delight of Michelangelo, who rushed to view it. It now stands in a recess of the charming octagonal Belvedere Courtyard.

> You'll find few labels on the works in the Vatican museums, but you can buy a detailed guide at the Vatican Tourist Office.

Roman copies of some other Greek sculptures, such as the *Aphrodite of Cnidos* by Praxiteles and the superb *Apollo Belvedere*, achieved a fame as great as the originals, which are now sadly lost. Take note in particular of the powerful muscular first-century B.C. *Torso* by Apollonius, which has had a profound influence on artists and sculptors to this day.

The **Gregorian-Etruscan Museum** displays the exciting finds from a seventh-century B.C. Etruscan burial mound at Cerveteri (see page 81), whose tomb yielded an abundance of treasures. Among the fine jewelry is a gold brooch curiously decorated with lions and ducklings. Look out for the striking bronze statue of a sprightly Etruscan warrior, the *Mars of Todi* (fourth century B.C.).

Judging by the number of obelisks scattered throughout Rome, Egyptian art was much admired and sought after by the ancient Romans. The basis of the collection in the **Egyptian Museum** rests on finds from Rome and its surroundings, particularly from the Gardens of Sallust between the Pincian and Quirinal hills, the Temple of Isis on the Campus Martius, and Hadrian's Villa at Tivoli (see page 77). One of the rooms recreates the underground chamber of a tomb in the Valley of the Kings.

Pope Julius II took a calculated risk in 1508 when he called in a relatively untried 26-year-old to decorate his new residence. The result was the four **Stanze di Raffaello** (the Raphael Rooms). In the central and most visited Stanza della Segnatura are the two masterly frescoes, *Dispute over the Holy Sacrament* and the famous *School of Athens*, which contrasted theological and philosophical wisdom. The *Disputation* unites biblical figures with historical pillars of the faith such as Pope Gregory, Thomas Aquinas, and others, including painter Fra Angelico and the divine Dante. At the center of the *School*, Raphael is believed to have given red-robed Plato the features of Leonardo da Vinci, while portraying Michelangelo as the thoughtful Heraclitus, seated in the foreground. Raphael himself appears in the lower right-hand corner.

For a stark contrast to Raphael's grand manner, seek out the gentle beauty of Fra Angelico's frescoes in the **Cappella del Beato Angelico** (Chapel of Nicholas V). The lives of saints Lawrence and Stephen are told in delicately subdued pinks and blues, highlighted with gold.

An incomparable endless array of treasures and antiquities is beautifully displayed at the renowned Vatican Museums.

The richly decorated **Borgia Apartments** contain Pinturicchio's sublime frescoes, with portraits of the Spanish Borgia Pope Alexander VI and his notorious son Cesare and daughter Lucrezia, and leads into the Collection of Modern Religious Art opened in 1973 by Paul VI. In this collection are Matisse's Madonna sketches, Rodin bronzes, Picasso ceramics, designs for ecclesiastical robes, and, somewhat unexpectedly, a grotesque pope by Francis Bacon.

One of Europe's finest collections of ancient manuscripts and rare books is kept in the hallowed precincts of the **Apostolic Library**. In the great vaulted reading room, or Sistine Hall, designed by Domenico Fontana in 1588, walls and ceilings are covered with paintings of ancient libraries, conclaves, thinkers, and writers. Showcases displaying precious illuminated manuscripts have replaced the old lecterns. A 1,600-year-old copy of Virgil's works, the poems of Petrarch, a sixth-century gospel of St. Matthew, and Henry VIII's love letters to Anne Boleyn are among the prize possessions.

Nothing can prepare you for the visual shock of the **Cappella Sistina** (Sistine Chapel), built for Sixtus IV in the 15th century. Restored to the original colors after a controversial ten-year restoration finished in 1990, the brightness and freshness of the frescoes are overwhelming. Despite the distracting presence of the hushed crowds, visitors seem to yield to the power of Michelangelo's ceiling, and his *Last Judgment*. The other wall frescoes, of Botticelli, Rosselli, Pinturicchio, Ghirlandaio, and Signorelli, are barely given a moment's notice. In this private papal chapel, where cardinals hold their conclaves to elect new popes, the glory of the Catholic Church achieves its finest artistic expression.

The chapel portrays nothing less than the story of man, in three parts: from Adam to Noah; the giving of the Law to Moses; and from the birth of Jesus to the Last Judgment.

Towards the center of the ceiling you can make out the celebrated outstretched finger of the *Creation of Adam*. Most overwhelming of all, particularly now that the colors are so fresh and vivid, is the impression of the whole. This is best appreciated looking back from the bench by the chapel's exit.

On the chapel's altar wall is Michelangelo's tempestuous *Last Judgment* (restored in 1994), finished 25 years after the ceiling's completion in 1512, when the artist was in his sixties, and imbued with profound religious soul-searching. An almost naked Jesus dispenses justice; he is more like a stern, even fierce classical god-hero than the conventionally gentle biblical figure. It is said that the artist's agonizing self-portrait can be seen in the flayed skin of St. Bartholomew, below Jesus.

Amid all the Vatican's treasures, the 15 rooms of the **Pinacoteca Vaticana** (Picture Gallery) in a separate wing of the palace, sometimes get short shrift. In this collection, covering nine centuries of painting, are important works by Fra Angelico,

Perugino, Raphael's *Transfiguration* (his last great work), Leonardo da Vinci's unfinished *St. Jerome* in somber tones of sepia, Bellini's *Pietà*, and Caravaggio's *Descent from the Cross*.

As you wander the galleries, glance out of the windows from time to time to view St. Peter's dome over the clipped hedges of the

Michelangelo spent four years painting the ceiling of the Sistine Chapel.

Vatican Gardens (the best views are from the Gallery of the Maps). Take a rest in the **Cortile della Pigna**, dominated by the enormous bronze pinecone fountain (first century A.D.) which gives the courtyard its name.

CHURCHES

With more than 250 churches within the center of the city, it's impossible to list — much less visit — all the churches in Rome. Students of history and art, as well as pilgrims, should aim to visit, at the very least, the four patriarchal basilicas: St. Peter's, Santa Maria Maggiore (the most visited after St. Peter's), St. John Lateran, and St. Paul's Outside the Walls.

Some churches have relics of saints and martyrs that make them special sites, while others are significant landmarks in the development of Western architecture, and many more contain magnificent works of art. Here is a representative selection of those that visitors will want to include in their itinerary (See page 117 in Travel Tips for open hours).

Santa Maria Maggiore

According to a 13th-century legend, this largest and most splendid of all the churches dedicated to the Virgin Mary was built in the fourth century by Pope Liberius after a vision from the Virgin Mary. In fact, it almost certainly dates from 420, and was completed soon afterwards by Pope Sixtus III.

Glittering **mosaics** enhance the perfect proportions of the interior. Above the 40 ancient Ionic columns of the triple nave, a mosaic frieze portrays Old Testament scenes leading to the coming of Christ. The theme is continued in the gilded Byzantine-style mosaics on the triumphal arch, detailing the birth and the childhood of Jesus, and culminates in the magnificent 13th-century portrayal of Mary and Jesus enthroned in the apse behind the high altar. Inlaid red and green pre-

The first gold shipped from the New World gilds the elaborate Renaissance ceiling of the Santa Maria Maggiore.

cious marbles pattern the floor in a style first pioneered by Rome's illustrious Cosmati family of craftsmen during the 12th century. Don't forget to look up — the basilica's glowing coffered ceiling by Giuliano San Gallo is said to be gilded with the first shipment of gold to arrive from the New World, a gift from the Spanish throne to the Pope.

The incomparably rich **Cappella Paolina** (Pauline Chapel) has an altar inlaid with agate, amethyst, and lapis lazuli set beneath a revered ninth-century painting of the Madonna and Child. On August 5, white petals are showered on the altar to mark the date when a miraculous fall of summertime snow, along with a vision of the Virgin, showed fourth-century Pope Liberius where to build the first church on this site.

St. John Lateran (San Giovanni in Laterano)

Regarded as the mother church of the Roman Catholic world (it's the seat of the Pope as bishop of Rome), **San Giovanni**

in Laterano predated even the first St. Peter's by a few years. Emperor Constantine built both basilicas in the early fourth century. The version you enter is the sixth or seventh structure rebuilt on this site.

> When visiting any church, shorts and tank tops (men and women), miniskirts, or backless dresses should not be worn.

Popes lived in the Lateran Palace for a thousand years until they moved to Avignon, and then to the Vatican upon their return to Rome in 1377. On a wooden table, incorporated in the high altar, St. Peter himself is said to have celebrated mass.

Fire, earthquake, and looting by the Vandals reduced the church to ruins over the centuries. The present basilica still uses the bronze central doors that graced the entrance to the Curia in the Forum in ancient Rome (see page 41). High above the basilica's facade, 15 giant white statues of Jesus, John the Baptist, and Church sages stand out against the sky.

Transformed by Borromini in the 17th century, the echoey interior of the church gives a predominant impression of somber white and gray, more restrained than is usual for Baroque architects. The only exuberant touches are the colored marble inlays of the paving and several statues of the Apostles which were sculpted by pupils of Bernini.

Site of the first Christian baptism in Rome, the **baptistery** preserves some truly splendid fifth- and seventh-century mosaics. The beautiful bronze doors of St. John the Baptist's Chapel, removed from the Baths of Caracalla (see page 49), sing musically on their hinges when they are opened (ask the custodian to oblige).

The brothers Jacopo and Pietro Vassalletto excelled themselves in the **cloisters**, where alternating straight and twisted columns, set in mosaic style, create a perfect setting for meditation.

An ancient edifice opposite the basilica — almost all that's left of the original Lateran Palace — shelters the **Scala Santa**, the holy stairway brought back by St. Helena from Jerusalem and said to have been trodden by Jesus in the house of Pontius Pilate (more likely, it was built here on this spot in the early fourth century by Pope Sylvester). The devout still climb the 28 marble steps on their knees. When Florence's Uffizi Galleries were damaged by a terrorist bomb in 1993, a similar act occurred in St. John Lateran immediately thereafter; visible remnants of restoration are still going on in the church.

Outside the basilica stands an Egyptian **obelisk** brought from the Temple of Ammon in Thebes. It's the tallest in the world — 32 m (102 ft.) — and, dating from the 15th century B.C., possibly the oldest of the 13 still standing in Rome.

St. Paul's Outside the Walls

St. Paul's Basilica, the largest in Rome after St. Peter's, was built by Constantine in A.D. 314 and enlarged by Valentinian II and Theodosius. Astonishingly, it survived intact until destroyed by fire in 1823. Today, a faithful restoration, though preserving only a little of its former splendor, has recreated **San Paolo Fuori le Mura**'s original form.

Massive Byzantine doors in decorative bronze panels that date to the 11th century survived the fire and now appear on the west wall. A **ciborium** (1285) attributed to the Florentine architect and sculptor Arnolfo di Cambio, retrieved from the ashes, decorates the high altar, under which lies the supposed burial place of St. Paul the Apostle. After Paul was beheaded, a Roman matron, Lucina, placed the body here in her family vault. Constantine later encased it in a sarcophagus of marble and bronze, looted by Saracen invaders later on.

Above the 86 Venetian marble columns runs a row of mosaic medallions representing all the popes, from St. Peter to the present day. Surviving the great fire, and one of the church's greatest draws, is the peaceful Benedictine **cloister**, designed by Pietro Vassalletto in the early 13th-century and surpassing even his work at St. John Lateran. Slender, spiraled columns glitter with green, red, and gold mosaic, enclosing a garden of roses and a gently rippling fountain.

San Clemente

This gem of a church hides a fascinating history which can be traced down through each of its three levels (a cross-section situation typical of Rome, but unusual in that the different levels here can be visited). The present church, dating to the 12th century, is built in basilica form with three naves divided by ancient columns and embellished by a pavement of geometric designs. A symbolic mosaic in the apse features the Cross as the Tree of Life nourishing all living things: birds, animals, and plants.

To the right of the nave, a staircase leads down to the fourth-century **basilica**, which underpins the present church. The Romanesque frescoes, unfortunately, have now drastically faded, but copies show them in the near-perfect condition in which they were uncovered earlier in the 20th century.

An ancient stairway leads farther underground to a maze of corridors and chambers, believed to be the home of St. Clement himself, third successor to St. Peter as pope and martyred by Hadrian in A.D. 88. Also down here is the earliest religious structure on this site, a second-century A.D. pagan **temple** (*Mithraeum*) dedicated to the god Mithras, the Persian god of light whose cult following once rivaled the early Catholic Church. A sculpture shows him slaying a bull.

San Pietro in Vincoli

Just south of Piazza Cavour, **St. Peter in Chains** might not attract a second glance if it didn't contain one of Michelangelo's greatest sculptures, his formidable ***Moses***. Intended for St. Peter's as part of Michelangelo's unsuccessful project for Julius II's tomb, the statue of the great biblical figure sits in awesome majesty at the center of the space. You can imagine how utterly grandiose the original plan for the tomb must have been when you realize that Moses was supposed to be just one of 40 figures adorning it (the plan was aborted when Julius decided he wanted Michelangelo to paint the Sistine Chapel instead). The "horns" on his head continue the traditional medieval mistranslation of the Hebrew for halo-like rays of light. A profile of Michelangelo is said to hide in Moses' flowing beard (hint: look below the lower lip). On each side, the comparatively passive figures of Jacob's two wives, a prayerful Rachel and melancholy Leah, were the last completed sculptures of Michelangelo.

Empress Eudoxia founded the church in the fifth century, on the site of the Roman law court where St. Peter was tried and sentenced. It was built as a sanctuary for the chains with which Herod bound St. Peter in Palestine, together with those used when he was imprisoned in Rome. They are kept in a bronze reliquary beneath the high altar.

The Gesù

Severe and relatively discreet, on its own piazza west of the Piazza Venezia, the Gesù is the mother church of the Jesuits and was a major element in their Counter-Reformation campaign. Begun as their Roman headquarters in 1568, its open plan became the model for the congregational churches that were intended to wrest popular support from the Protestants. While its facade is more sober than the Baroque churches put up as the movement gained momentum, the interior glorifies the new-found militancy in gleaming bronze, gold, marble, and precious stones.

St. Ignatius Loyola, a Spanish soldier who founded the order, has a fittingly magnificent **tomb** under a richly decorated altar in the left transept, with a rich profusion of lapis lazuli (which is actually a thin shell fused to plaster stucco).

Sant'Ignazio

In gentler contrast, the nearby 17th-century church of Sant'Ignazio stands in an enchanting setting of russet and ochre Rococo houses. Inside, Fra Andrea Pozzo (himself a Jesuit priest and designer of the saint's tomb in the Gesù) has painted a superb *trompe-l'oeil* **ceiling fresco** (1685) depicting St. Ignatius's entry into paradise. Stand on a buff stone disk in the nave's central aisle and you will have the extraordinary impression of the whole building rising above you through the ingenious architectural effect of the painting. From any other point, the columns appear to collapse. From another disk farther up the aisle you can admire the celestial dome above the unmissable Baroque altar, but as you advance, the dome begins to take on strange proportions. The church is known for its elaborate Christmas nativity.

MUSEUMS

The Romans have been enthusiastic patrons and collectors of art for millennia, and their museums are packed with treasures. Here are a few of the best, in addition to the Vatican Museums (see page 57).

Galleria Borghese

The avid and ruthless art collector Cardinal Scipione Borghese conceived this handsome Baroque villa in the Villa Borghese park (see page 28) as a home for his small but outstanding collection, using his prestige as the nephew of Pope Paul V to extort coveted masterpieces from their owners.

Despite the inevitable stiff neck, you can't help but keep your eyes heavenward when visiting the Galleria Borghese.

After an extensive 14-year restoration, the Borghese reopened to much fanfare, with its entire collection on view, in spring of 1997. It is one of Italy's loveliest small museums.

The highlights of the collection are several astonishing **sculptures** by the cardinal's young protégé, Bernini. These include busts of his patron; a vigorous *David* (said to be a youthful self-portrait); and a graceful nearby sculpture, *Apollo and Daphne*, in which the 26-year-old sculptor depicted the water nymph turning into a laurel just as the god is about to seize her. A later addition, now the star attraction, is Antonio Canova's portrayal of Napoleon's sister Pauline, who married into the Borghese family, as a naked reclining Venus (1805).

There are some exceptional pieces in the collection, including Raphael's masterful *Deposition*; Titian's *Sacred and Profane Love*; a number of Caravaggio's works, including *David with the Head of Goliath* and the *Madonna of the Serpent* (Cardinal

Borghese was one of the artist's earliest sponsors); along with works by Botticelli, Rubens, Dürer, and Cranach.

Villa Giulia

This 16th-century pleasure palace built for Pope Julius III (partially designed by Vasari) in the northwest area of the Villa Borghese park, is now the lovely setting for Italy's finest **Etruscan Museum**. Although much about this pre-Roman civilization is still a mystery, the Etruscans (found in Tuscany and Umbria, and in parts of Lazio, north of Rome) left a wealth of detail about their customs and everyday life by burying the personal possessions of the dead with them in their tombs.

Replicas show the round stone burial mounds, built like huts. Room after room is filled with objects from the tombs: bronze statues of warriors in battledress; shields, weapons, and chariots (even the skeletons of two horses); gold and silver jewelry; decorative vases imported by Etruscans from Greece; and a host of everyday cooking utensils, mirrors, and combs. Note the bronze toilet box adorned with figures of the Argonauts. The museum's highlight is a life-size terra-cotta sixth-century B.C. sculpture for a sarcophagus lid, depicting a blissful young couple reclining on a banquet couch.

Museo Nazionale Romano

Major reconstruction, finished in 1998, has showcased the extensive collection of art works of the Museo Nazionale Romano, many of which could not previously be shown to the public for lack of space. It has now been divided between three separate sites: the Baths of Diocletian, Palazzo Altemps, and (the most visited) Palazzo Massimo.

The part housed in the Roman **Baths of Diocletian** offers a compulsory introduction to Rome's Greek and Roman antiquities. Larger even than those of Caracalla, Diocletian's baths covered 120 hectares (300 acres), part of which are now occupied by the Piazza della Repubblica and Michelangelo's church of Santa Maria degli Angeli, near Termini station.

But the newly opened **Palazzo Altemps** features the magnificent **Ludovisi**, **Brancaccio**, **Del Drago**, and **Mattei collections** in a gorgeous 16th-century setting. Among the most important pieces is the marble altartop known as the *Ludovisi Throne*, an original Greek work from the fifth century B.C., with exquisitely carved reliefs of Aphrodite and a maiden playing the flute. Also seek out the tragic statue of a Barbarian warrior in the act of killing himself and his wife rather than submit to slavery. Other highlights include the *Apollo of the Tiber*, a copy of a bronze group by the young Pheidias; a copy (probably the best ever) of Myron's famed *Discobolos* (Discus Thrower); the *Daughter of Niobe*, an original from the fifth century B.C.; the *Venus of Cyrene*; a bronze of a young man leaning on a lance; and a variety of portrait sculptures, including one of Emperor Augustus. Autoguide rentals will talk you through the beautifully displayed collections.

Antiquities buffs may be most impressed by the 19th-century **Palazzo Massimo**, home to the landscape frescoes taken from the imperial villa of Livia, which show nature at its most bountiful, with flowers, trees, birds, and fruit painted with great attention to detail. There is also a collection of ancient Roman jewelry, and an extensive coin collection from the republic and imperial eras up until the Renaissance as well as today's Italian lire and tomorrow's euro. Guided tours in English of Palazzo Massimo (L6,000) depart regularly.

Galleria Nazionale d'Arte Antica

The Palazzo Barberini (on the Via delle Quattro Fontane) provided another architectural battleground for rivals Borro-

mini and Bernini, each of whom built one of its grand stair-
cases and contributed to the superb facade. It is worth a visit
as much for its Baroque decor as for its collection of 13th to
17th century paintings in the National Gallery of Ancient
Art. Don't forget to look up in the Salone or **Great Hall** for
Pietro da Cortona's dazzling illusionist ceiling fresco, *Tri-
umph of Divine Providence* (1633–1639).

Most of the national art collection is hung in the first-floor
gallery (the rest is housed in the **Palazzo Corsini** across the
Tiber in Trastevere). Works include a Fra Angelico triptych,
the famous portrait of King Henry VIII by Hans Holbein, and
paintings by Titian, Tintoretto, and El Greco. Two stars among
many are Raphael's *La Fornarina* (The Baker's Daughter),
said to be a portrait of his mistress and model for many of his
madonnas, and Caravaggio's depiction of Judith in the act of
severing the head of Holofernes.

Galleria Doria Pamphili

The vast Palazzo Doria off the Piazza Venezia, the private residence of the important Doria family, has recently been
opened to the public. The family's rich collection of paintings
was assembled over hundreds of years. A catalog is vital, as
in the jigsaw display, paintings are identified by number.

Much of the collection is poorly lit, but there are a number of masterpieces from the 15th to the 17th century,
including works by Titian, Veronese, Tintoretto, Raphael,
and master works by Caravaggio, as well as paintings from
the Dutch and Flemish schools. Look out for the evocative
landscape of the *Flight into Egypt* by Annibale Carracci
and the windswept *Naval Battle in the Bay of Naples* by
Brueghel the Elder.

You'll find a nice stylistic contrast in a little room off the
galleries: a brilliant worldly portrait by Velázquez of

Innocent X, the Pamphili family pope alongside a more serene marble bust of him by Bernini.

Art Center ACEA Montemartini

Rome's newest concession to industrial-chic is a bit out-of-the-way between Trastevere and Ostiense (Via Ostiense, 106; Tel. 06-5748030). This former electrical power station has been converted into a fascinating museum which juxtaposes industrial machinery with more than 400 classic Roman statues taken from the Capitoline Museum, where they could not be displayed for lack of space. Open hours are Tuesday to Friday, 10am to 6pm (to 7pm weekends; admission L12,000).

EXCURSIONS

☛ Old Appian Way

Don't miss visiting the Via Appia Antica, the Old Appian Way, just outside the city walls. Heading southeast through the Porta San Sebastiano, look back for a good view of the old **Aurelian Wall**, still enclosing part of Rome. Its massive defensive ramparts stretch into the distance, topped by towers and bastions built to resist the onslaught of Barbarian invasions in the third century.

Ahead lies a narrow lane, hemmed in at first by hedges and the high walls of film stars' and millionaires' homes — the **Old Appian Way**. When Appius Claudius the Censor opened the consular road and gave it his name in 312 B.C., the Appian Way was the first of the great Roman roads. You can still see some of the original paving stones over which the Roman legions marched 370 km (222 miles) on their way to coastal Brindisi to set sail for the Levant and North Africa.

By law, burials could not take place within the city walls, so on either side of the road lie the ruins of sepulchres of 20

***All roads once led to Rome, and the historical proof
exists throughout the Italian countryside.***

generations of patrician Roman families, some with simple tablets, others with impressive mausoleums.

At a fork in the road, the 17th-century chapel of **Domine Quo Vadis** marks the spot where St. Peter, fleeing Nero's persecution, is said to have encountered Christ and asked: "*Domine, quo vadis?*" ("Whither goest thou, Lord?"). Christ is believed to have replied: "I go to Rome to be crucified again." Ashamed of his fear, Peter turned back to Rome and his own crucifixion. The little chapel contains a copy of a stone with a footprint said to have been left by Jesus (the original is in the Basilica of San Sebastiano).

Farther along the Appia Antica, within a short distance of each other, are three of Rome's most celebrated **catacombs**: San Domitilla, St. Callisto (the largest and the most famous), and St. Sebastian. Millions of early Christians, among them many martyrs and saints, were buried in 50 of these vast cemeteries. Knowledgeable guides accompany groups into a labyrinth of damp, musty-smelling tunnels and chambers burrowed into the soft volcanic tufa rock, sometimes six levels deep (the claustrophobic should abstain). Paintings and carvings adorn the catacombs with precious examples of early Christian art.

San Domitilla is the oldest and perhaps the most enjoyable to visit. The entrance to the **Catacombs of San Callisto** lies at the end of an avenue of cypresses. An official tour takes you down to the second level of excavations, where you will see the burial niches, called *loculi*, cut into the rock one above

The Third City

The historic center of Rome has been kept mercifully free of antagonistic turn-of-the-millennium innovations. But there is an modern-day "Third Rome" 5 km (3 miles) south along the Ostian Way. This was Mussolini's dream, intended to rival the glories of the Imperial and Renaissance cities.

Known simply by its initials EUR (pronounced "Ay-oor"), this complex of massive white-marble buildings of fascist design, with wide avenues and open spaces grouped around an artificial lake, was designed for a world fair in 1942, that was intended to mark 20 years of Fascism. The war interrupted construction, however, and the fair never took place.

In recent years, EUR has developed into a thriving township of government ministries, offices, conference centers, and fashionable apartments. Several buildings remain from Mussolini's time, including the formidable cube of arches of the Palazzo della Civiltà del Lavoro (Palace of Workers), known as the "Square Colosseum." For the 1960 Olympics, engineer Pier Luigi Nervi and architect Marcella Piacentini designed the huge, domed Palazzo dello Sport.

the other on either side of the dark galleries. Occasionally the narrow passages open out into larger chambers, or *cubicula*, where a family would be buried together. More than ten early popes were buried here; so was St. Cecilia until she was transferred to the church of Santa Cecilia in Trastevere (the statue of the saint lying in a recess is a copy of the one by Stefano Maderno in the church; see page 39). In the **Catacombs of San Sebastiano**, the bodies of the apostles Peter and Paul are said to have been hidden for several years during the third-century persecutions. You can still see graffiti in Latin and Greek invoking the two saints.

The cylindrical **tomb of Cecilia Metella** dominates the Appian landscape. This noblewoman was the wife of the immensely rich Crassus, who financed Julius Caesar's early campaigns. In 1302 the Roman owners added the towers and battlements when they turned it into their fortified castle.

Alongside extends the well-preserved **Circus of Maxentius**, built for chariot races in A.D. 309 under the last pagan emperor. Turn off the Via Appia to visit the poignant memorial of **Fosse Ardeatine**, a place of pilgrimage for modern Italians. In March 1944, in retaliation for the killing of 32 German soldiers by the Italian Resistance, the Nazis rounded up at random 335 Italian men (10 for each German and an extra 15 for good measure) and machine-gunned them in the sandpits of the Via Ardeatina.

Tivoli

The picturesque town of Tivoli perches on a steep slope amid the woods, streams, and twisted silvery olive trees of the Sabine Hills. Inhabited even in ancient times, when it was known as *Tibur*, Tivoli prospered throughout the Middle Ages. It preserves interesting Roman remains, as well as medieval churches and its famous Renaissance villa and gardens.

The entrance and fountains of the Villa d'Este are reflected in one of many still pools.

Trains leave Stazione Termini every five minutes for Rebibbia terminal (metro line B). Buses make the connection from there to Tivoli. By car the drive takes 45 minutes (30 km/19 miles) along the old Roman chariot road (since repaved!) of the Via Tiburtina; or take the A4 Autostrada direction Aquila and exit at Tivoli.

The **Villa d'Este** sprawls along the hillside. From its balconies you can look down on its fabled gardens (the real reason for your visit), which fall away in a series of terraces — a paradise of dark cypresses, umbrella pines, fountains (estimated at 500), artificial grottoes, pools, and statues.

Cardinal Ippolito II d'Este conceived this modest villa and garden in 1550 (other gardens were added as recently as the early 20th century); the architect Piero Ligorio created it. On the **Terrace of 100 Fountains** water jets splash into a long basin guarded by statues of eagles. The **Organ Fountain**, originally accompanied by organ music, cascades steeply down the rocks. On the lowest level three large, still pools contrast with the rush and roar of water elsewhere. The architect took particular delight in strange fantasies, such as the rows of sphinxes who spurt water from their nipples.

Down the road (5 km/3 miles), tucked away at the foot of the hills, lie the haunting ruins of **Villa Adriana** (Hadrian's Villa). Spread over 70 hectares (173 acres), this retirement hideaway of the great builder of the Pantheon and Hadrian's

Wall in England was one of the most extravagant constructed during ancient times, designed to recapture some of the architectural marvels of his empire. The countless treasures that filled his pleasure palace have since found their way to museums around the world.

Those arriving at the villa by public bus are dropped off at the main gate and ticket office. Tourist coaches and private cars continue up the drive to the parking lot on the grounds. An excellent scale model here will give you an overview of the whole. As you will see, this was more a miniature resort village than a villa. The monumental baths, separate Greek and Latin libraries (areas where guests reclined while eating), temples, and pavilions together make up the home of a man who drew no distinction between the pleasures of mind and body.

You enter the ruins through the colonnades of the Greek-style **Stoa Poikile** (Painted Portico), which leads to the main imperial residence. Adjoining the palace are guest rooms, their black-and-white mosaic floors still visible, and an underground passageway through which the servants moved about unseen.

The enchanting **Teatro Marittimo**, a pavilion surrounded by a little reflecting pool and circular portico, epitomizes all the magic of the place. To the south, remnants of arches and copies of Greek-style caryatids (statues of females used as pillars) surround the **Pool of Canopus** leading to the sanctuary of the Egyptian god Serapis. Barbarians and museum curators have removed most of the villa's treasures, but a stroll among the remaining pillars, arches, and mosaics in gardens running wild among the olive trees, cypresses, and umbrella pines can be wonderfully evocative of a lost world. Two small on-site museums help recreate the emperor's retreat in its day.

Ostia Antica

Excavations continue to uncover fascinating sections of what was once the seaport and naval base of Rome when it was the most important city in the Western world. The long-buried city of Ostia stands at the mouth (*ostium*) of the Tiber, 23 km (14 miles) southwest of the capital on the shores of the Tyrrhenian Sea — a convenient and enjoyable substitute for those not visiting Pompei.

Sea-going vessels were unable to travel inland along the shallow Tiber, so river barges plied back and forth from the port, carrying imperial Rome's supply of food and building materials. During its heyday, the once prosperous port city had 100,000 residents and boasted two splendid public baths, a theater (where plays are still occasionally offered), many temples, and the villas of wealthy merchants.

Ostia's well-preserved ruins, set among cypresses and pines (bring a picnic and enjoy a cool respite) may reveal more about daily life and the building methods of ancient Rome than do those of the capital. Excavations since the 19th century have unearthed Ostia's **Decumanus Maximus** (Main Street) and a grid of side streets, lined with warehouses, apartments known as *insulae* (islands), and private houses facing out to sea and decorated with mosaics and murals.

The **Piazzale delle Corporazioni** (Square of the Corporations) housed 70 commercial offices round a porticoed central temple to Ceres, goddess of agriculture. Mosaic mottoes and emblems in the pavement tell of the trading of grain factors, caulkers, ropemakers, and shipowners from all over the world. The **theater** next door, built by Agrippa, is worth the climb up the tiered seats that accommodated 2,700, for a panoramic view over the whole ruined city.

As in Rome, the **Forum** was the focus of city life, dominated at one end by the Capitol, a temple dedicated to Jupiter, Juno, and Minerva, and at the other by the Temple of Rome and Augustus, with the Curia (seat of the municipal authorities) and the basilica, or law courts, lying in between.

To see a typical residence, visit the **House of Cupid and Psyche** with its rooms paved in marble and built round a central garden courtyard. Nearby a small on-site **museum** traces Ostia's history through statues, busts, and frescoes.

The modern seaside resort of Lido di Ostia attracts weekending Romans, who flock to the gray-sand beaches. Swimming is not recommended because of pollution, but most beach establishments have swimming pools. There are many terraced bars and restaurants where you can have lunch or a snack.

Cerveteri

If the Villa Giulia in Rome (see page 71) and the Gregorian-Etruscan Museum in the Vatican (see page 50) have aroused your curiosity about the pre-Roman Etruscans, it is worth making a trip to the ancient **necropolis** at Cerveteri, 43 km (27 miles) northwest of Rome. Known in ancient times as *Caere*, it was one of the original 12 towns of the powerful Etruscan League, though it declined in the third century B.C. after becoming a Roman dependency.

The scores of **tombs** here represent every kind of burial, from the early shaft and pit graves to *tumuli*, dating from the seventh to first centuries B.C. Stucco decorations and rock carvings represent the weapons, domestic animals, and even household pots and pans that Etruscans felt they would need in the afterlife.

The **Museo Nazionale di Cerveteri**, housed in a 16th-century castle, displays chronologically a rich collection of objects from the tombs, including sarcophagi, sculptures, and wall paintings.

Rome's Highlights

Note: Hours indicated here may change after the Jubilee year; check with the tourism office.

Castel Sant'Angelo. Lungotevere Castello 50; Tel. 06-39080730. Rome's greatest military bastion since A.D. 130, and the popes' refuge in troubled times. Open 9am–8pm Tues–Sun. L10,000.

Colosseo. Piazza Colosseo; Tel. 06-39749907. Where the ancient Roman games took place. Open 9am–5pm Mon–Sun. L10,000.

Domus Aurea. Viale della Domus Aurea; Tel. 06-39749907. Nero's "Golden House," recently reopened. Open 9am–8pm Mon–Sun. L12,000.

Foro Romano. Via del Foro Romano. Ancient Rome's governmental and religious center. Open 9am–5pm Mon–Sat (2pm Sunday). Admission free to Forum, L12,000.

Galleria Borghese. Piazza le Scipione Borghese 5; Tel. 06-32810. This small but outstanding collection was recently reopened to the public. Open 9am–8pm Tues–Fri (until midnight Sat, until 8pm Sun). L12,000.

Galleria Doria Pamphili. Piazza del Collegio Romano 2; Tel. 06-6797323 A collection of paintings assembled over centuries by the Doria family. Open 10am–5pm; closed Thurs. L13,000.

Musei Capitolini. Piazza del Campidoglio; Tel. 06-67102071. A magnificent collection of ancient Roman sculpture and a small but significant collection of paintiings in the Campidoglio palaces. Open 9am–7pm; closed Mon L10,000. Last Sun of month free.

Museo Etrusco di Villa Giulia. Piazzale Villa Giulia 9; Tel. 06-3201951. The finest Etruscan Museum in Italy. Open 9am–7pm Tues–Sat (8pm Sun). L8,000.

Musei Vaticani. Viale Vaticano; Tel. 06-69883860. The treasures in the Vatican Museums offer a microcosm of Western art and civilization. Open 8:45am–1:45pm Mon–Fri (12:45pm Sat). L15,000. Open last Sun of month, free (and crowded).

Palazzo Altemps (Museo Nazionale Romano). Piazza S. Apollinare 44; Tel. 06-39749907. In a newly opened 16th-century palazzo, important exhibits include the famous Ludovisi collection. Open 9am–6:45pm Tues–Sat (7:45pm Sun). L10,000.

Palazzo Barberini (Museo Nazionale D'Arte Antica). Via Barberini18; Tel. 06-32810. The art collection is worth visiting for the setting alone. Open 9am–7pm; closed Mon. L12,000.

Palazzo Venezia. Via del Plebiscito118; Tel. 06-69994318. Rome's first great Renaissance palace. Open 9am–1:30pm Tues–Sat (1pm Sun). L8,000.

Pantheon. Piazza della Rotonda. Rome's best preserved ancient monument, built in A.D. 125. Open 9am–6:30pm Mon–Sat (1pm Sunday). Admission free.

Piazza Navona. A place of recreation since Roman times, centered by Bernini's Fountain of the Four Rivers, it's the best place in Rome for people-watching and street entertainment.

Piazza di Spagna. One of Rome's best known landmarks, the three tiers of the famous Spanish Steps ascend from the piazza to a Baroque church. Rome's most popular meeting place for Romans and visitors alike.

St. Peter's Basilica. Piazza San Pietro. Bernini's great square is an exciting setting for the world's primary (and largest) Roman Catholic Church. Open daily 7am–6pm (June–Sept until 7pm). Admission free.

Santa Maria Maggiore. Piazza Santa Maria Maggiore; Tel. 06-4881094. The most splendid of the churches dedicated to the Virgin Mary, begun in the fourth century. Open daily 7am–7pm. Admission free.

Terme di Caracalla. Viale Terme di Caracalla 52; Tel. 06-39749907. These vast ancient Roman baths once accommodated 1,600 people. Open 9am–5pm Tues–Sat (2pm Sun, 1:45pm Mon). L8,000.

WHAT TO DO

ENTERTAINMENT

Rome offers a wealth of evening entertainment, particularly in the summer months when the balmy evenings entice everyone outdoors. You can choose from the hottest of discos and nightclubs to the coolest of classical music, not to mention lively street festivals full of dancing, fireworks, and open-air dining. Rome's popular summer festival, *L'Estate Romana*, runs from June to September and offers music, film, dance, and theater in venues across the city, many of them open air and often free of charge.

The best known venue for **classical music** is the Accademia Nazionale di Santa Cecilia (Via della Conciliazione; Tel. 06-68801044), which presents symphonic, chamber music, and instrumental recitals from October to May. Concerts of classical music are also performed in a number of picturesque and historic settings, including the Campidoglio (see page 23), the Isola Tiberina (see page 37), and the cloister of Santa Maria della Pace. Military and civilian bands perform **free concerts** in the Pincio Gardens (see page 28) from late April to mid-July.

Opera and ballet are presented at the Teatro dell'Opera (Piazza Gigli at Via Torino; Tel. 06-481601). The opera season runs from November to late spring, with ballet presented in the other months. Once the ruins of the Baths of Caracalla (see page 49) were the spectacular location for a summer season of opera and ballet, something the tourism authorities hope to bring back.

Music clubs also abound in Rome, with all kinds of music, ranging from jazz, blues, and folk to rock, reggae, and salsa. The major live venue for jazz is Alexanderplatz (via

Ostia, 9; Tel. 06-39-742171; closed Monday). Blues and some jazz are found at Big Mama, on a tiny side street in Trastevere (Vicolo San Francesco a Ripa, 18; Tel. 06-5812551); call for the schedule.

Cinemas will usually dub foreign-language films into Italian. Exceptions are the Pasquino, the Quirinetta, the Alcazar (on Mondays) and the Nuovo Olimpia.

For up-to-the-minute information about what's going on in Rome, consult the entertainment supplement, *Trovaroma*, in the Thursday edition of *La Repubblica* newspaper, and the weekly *Roma C'è* and *Time Out*. The *Carnet di Roma* is a monthly guide to events in and around the city, produced by Rome's Tourist Board (see page 123). Sometimes even major events aren't confirmed until close to the last minute.

SHOPPING

Italian fashions and products from its gifted artisans are extremely popular and it's not unusual to buy a suitcase to take home the goodies. Real bargains can be found during sales (January and July).

IVA (value-added tax) is incorporated into prices on a sliding scale, going up as high as 19 percent. Non-EU citizens are entitled to a refund of this tax on purchases of L350,000 or more, if made in one place; request an invoice from the seller.

Getting Tickets

A centralized booking number for advance purchase of tickets (from overseas) for major museums is in the working; this will eliminate the high-season lines at the Vatican Museums and the Galleria Borghese (check with your hotel when booking). In the meantime, try the web site **www.romagiubileo.it**, which hopes to stay open after 2000, where you can book a number of different museums, theaters, and events.

Save your receipts until you leave your last EU destination. If you are leaving from Rome, remember to take your receipts to

| Look for a sign: *saldi* — on sale. |

be stamped *before* you check in. Watch for shops with a sign, TAX-FREE SHOPPING FOR TOURISTS. These stores will usually deduct the IVA on the spot.

Where to Shop

The most fashionable (and expensive) shopping district in Rome lies between Piazza di Spagna and Via del Corso. The best in high fashion, jewelry, fabrics, and leather is available in elegant shops on Via Condotti and its neighboring side streets: Via Borgognona, Via Frattina, and Via Bocca di Leone. Stroll from Piazza di Spagna to Piazza del Popolo on Via del Babuino for other famous-name boutiques.

Via Cola di Rienzo, just across the river is not so exclusive but its stores offer good, sometimes excellent quality. Via Nazionale and Via del Tritone are less expensive places to shop for both fashionable clothes and leather.

Specialist shops, which are often family-run and generations old, are the rule in Rome. You won't find the number of grand department stores boasted by other capital cities. The best of Rome's few big stores are Coin (Piazzale Appio, near St. John Lateran) and La Rinascente (main branch at Piazza Colonna on Via del Corso). The Standa and Upim chains, with branches throughout the city, often have the latest looks, of lesser quality and more accessible prices. They are usually open at lunchtime.

Be prepared to haggle if you go to Porta Portese, Rome's famous **flea market** held on Sunday morning in the streets and alleys running beside Via Portuense in Trastevere. Here you will find new and old clothes, antique bric-à-brac, furniture, jewelry, and books, as well as the odd pickpocket, so take care. And go for the color, if not to shop.

Italy is known for its art — don't underestimate the work that has yet to make it to the Vatican Museums!

The large **outdoor market** in Via Sannio (near St. John Lateran) is good for bargain clothes (every morning except Sunday). Piazza Vittorio Emanuele II (near Santa Maria Maggiore) has a colourful food market as well as stalls selling clothes and fabrics.

What to Buy

Antiques: It's no surprise to find antiques dealers by the score in a city 2,700 years old. Rome's dealers sell exquisite (but expensive) silver, glass, porcelain, furniture, and paintings. The best antiques shops are on Via del Babuino and Via Margutta (between the Spanish Steps and the Piazza del Popolo), Via Giulia (behind Palazzo Farnese), and Via dei Coronari (near Piazza Navona).

Buy antiques or art works only from a reputable dealer, i.e. one who will provide a certificate of guarantee and obtain the necessary government permit for export.

Books and prints: The open-air market at Largo Fontanella Borghese (off Via del Corso) specializes in original and reproduction prints and books.

Ceramics: Colorful, attractively designed carafes, plates, bowls, and tiles are available. Myricae in Via Frattina is good for reasonably priced regional handicrafts.

Fashion: Rome rivals Europe's major cities for stylish high-fashion clothes. All the famous names of Italian *alta moda* are represented in the Piazza di Spagna area. Fendi and Valentino are Rome's local stars, but you'll find all their peers: Armani, Etro, Krizia, Prada, Missoni, Versace, Gucci, and Max Mara.

You'll also find elegantly tailored men's clothes, both custom-made (you'll need to be around for various fittings)

It's not just togas and sandals anymore — the shops in Rome feature the finest of made-in-Italy fashion.

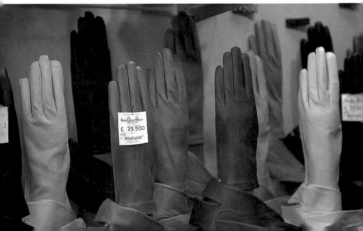

and ready-to-wear. La Cicogna, which has branches throughout the city, provides beautiful clothes for children.

Food and wine: Good gastronomic delicacies to take home with you include cheese (fresh Parmesan), salami, the Parma and San Daniele ham (*prosciutto crudo*), extra virgin olive oil, wines from the Castelli Romani, and fiery *grappa*. (Note that meat products cannot be brought into the US.)

Ai Monasteri in Piazza delle Cinque Lune (near Piazza Navona) sells handsomely packaged liqueurs, confectionery, olive oil, honey, and other products made by a number of different Italian monasteries.

Jewelry: You'll find fine antique jewelry in Rome, as well as modern design and costume jewelry. For sheer opulence, nothing can quite match the elegant, newly redecorated premises of Bulgari in Via Condotti.

Leather: Stylish leather goods — shoes, handbags, wallets, luggage, and gloves — abound. You'll find the likes of Ferragamo and Gucci in Via Condotti.

Textiles: Beautiful silks, colorful knitwear, and hand-embroidered table linens are supplied by Rome's shops. For textiles, go to the Via Tritone, which runs from Via del Corso northeast to the Via Veneto.

CHILDREN'S ROME

Children love Rome's fountains, especially throwing coins into the Fontana di Trevi. They also enjoy the slightly creepy feeling of putting their hands into the Bocca della Verità (see page 38). Children like visiting the catacombs (see page 75), and the horse and buggy rides in the Piazza Pantheon (also known as the Piazza Rotonda) are always popular.

Be sure to take your children to the Piazza Navona, where you will find all sorts of performers and other street-life entertainment: magicians, portrait artists, silhouette cutters,

and charicaturists. Also on the piazza is the best **toy store** in
Rome — Al Sogno (no. 53), which means "Dream," and is a
real dream for kids. Its two stories are chockablock with
made-in-Italy toys that can become instant heirlooms. And
don't forget the many *gelaterie*, where ice cream comes in
multiple exotic flavors; cones begin at about L2,500.

Calendar of Events

January 5–6 *Befana.* Epiphany festival in Piazza Navona.

January 21 Blessing of the Lambs. At Sant'Agnese, Via
Nomentana.

February/March *Carnivale.* Period preceding Lent;
masked processions and parades.

March 9 *Festa di San Francesco Romano.* Blessing at Piazzale del Colosseo.

March-April Good Friday. Pope leads the Procession of the
Cross at 9pm from the candlelit Colosseum to the Forum.
Easter Sunday, Pope blesses the crowds from the balcony of
St. Peter's at noon.

April-May *Festa della Primavera.* Spring Festival.

April 21 Founding of Rome.

June 29 *Festa di San Pietro e San Paolo.* Solemn rites in St.
Peter's Square.

July (last 2 weeks) *Noiantri.* Festival in Trastevere.

August 5 *Festa della Madonna della Neve.* Celebrated
in Santa Maria Maggiore.

August 15 *Ferragosto.* Feast of the Assumption.

September Open-air art exhibition in Via Margutta.

December Cultural Heritage Week. Free admission to
state museums and monuments (first week).
Children's toy fair. On Piazza Navona (until Jan. 6).

December 8 *Festa della Madonna Immacolata.* Immacu-
late Conception.

December 24 Christmas Eve midnight mass celebrated
by Pope in St. Peter's Basilica.

EATING OUT

For Italians, sitting down at the table and enjoying a meal together has always been a celebration. Until the booming sixties, Italy was basically an agricultural economy, and meat or lasagna were treats for Sunday. When eating out, Italians like to spend hours at the table, chatting with their family and friends and drinking wine. Now that traffic has been banned from large sections of Rome's historic center, outdoor dining on balmy summer evenings can be a delight. The area around Campo dei Fiori and nearby Piazza Navona (see page 32) has become what Via Veneto was during the days of the "dolce vita" — a place to while away the evening, first at one of the many restaurants, and later at an outdoor café. Other dining spots are Trastevere (see page 38), and the old Jewish ghetto (see page 36). Try to go out at least once into the countryside beyond the walls to eat in one of the restaurants along the Via Appia Antica, Tivoli, or Ostia (see page 80).

Restaurants must display the menu with prices in the window or just inside the door, so you will have an idea of what's offered before you take the plunge.

By law all restaurants (and bars) must issue a receipt or slip from the cash register indicating that the IVA (value added tax) has been included (you can be stopped and asked to show a receipt). The bill usually includes service (*servizio*) but ask if you're not sure. To avoid any complications, give your bill a look over before paying.

Where to Eat

Some hotels, usually the larger ones, serve an English- or American-style breakfast. Otherwise, go to a good *caffè* and settle for the *prima colazione* of superb coffee, *espresso*

Pick up some fresh fruit at a stall on the street — man cannot live on gelati alone... or can he?

(black) or *cappuccino* (with foaming hot milk), accompanied by a delicious sweet *cornetto* (croissant). Remember that in a bar what you consume will cost twice as much sitting at a table as standing at the bar.

For a quick snack at lunchtime, choose a *tavola calda*, a stand-up bar serving a variety of hot and cold dishes to take away or eat on the spot. Many bars offer the *tramezzino* unique to Rome — half a sandwich on loaf bread containing tuna, chicken, or egg salad, *prosciutto,* smoked salmon, or other ingredients. Or try having sandwiches made at a local delicatessen (*alimentari*). Ask for *panino ripieno*, a bread roll filled with sausage, ham, cheese, or salad.

Fast food and ethnic restaurants have increased considerably. Chinese restaurants abound, but you can also try African, Arab, Greek, Indian, Japanese, Lebanese, and Mexican cuisines. Vegetarian restaurants are gaining in popularity.

In theory, a *ristorante* is usually a larger and more elaborate establishment than a family-style *trattoria* or rustic *osteria*. But in Rome the distinction is blurred beyond all recognition.

Price should not be taken as an indication of the quality of cuisine — an expensive restaurant may offer a superb meal with service to match, but you pay for the location. Near famous tourist spots such as Piazza del Popolo and Piazza Navona, you'll find *trattorie* with lower prices where the ambience is much more appealing and the food has real character. While some restaurants offer fixed-price, three-course meals (*menù turistico* or *prezzo fisso*) which will save money, you'll almost always get better food by ordering individual dishes.

> When you enter a restaurant, shop, or office, the expected greeting is *buon giorno* (good morning) or *buona sera* (good evening) which is used beginning just after lunch.

Roman restaurants serve lunch from 12:30 to 3pm and dinner from 8 to 11pm. Some offer late-night supper and are open until 1 or even 2am. Restaurants are usually closed one day a week, which varies. It is always better to book by telephone, especially for peak hours (around 1:30pm and 9pm).

What to Eat

Antipasti: Any *trattoria* worth its olive oil will set out an artistic display of its antipasti (*hors d'oeuvre*) on a long table near the entrance. You can make your choices and fill your plate. Both attractive and tasty are the cold *peperoni*: red, yellow, and green peppers grilled, skinned, and marinated in olive oil and lemon juice. Mushrooms (*funghi*), artichokes (*carciofi*), and fennel (*finocchio*) come cold with a dressing (*pinzimonio*). One of the most refreshing antipasti is *mozzarella alla caprese*, slices of soft *mozzarella* cheese and tomato with fresh basil and olive oil. Ham from Parma or

San Daniele is paper thin, served with melon (*prosciutto con melone*) or, even better, fresh figs (*con fichi*).

Soups: Popular soups are vegetable (*minestrone*), clear soup (*brodo*), and a light version with an egg beaten into it (*stracciatella*).

Pasta: Traditionally served as an introductory course, not the main dish. Even the friendliest of restaurant owners will raise a sad eyebrow if you decide to make a whole meal out of a plate of spaghetti. There are supposedly as many different forms of Italian pasta as there are French cheeses — 360 at the last count, with new forms created every year. Each sauce — tomato, cheese, cream, meat, or fish — needs its own noodle.

Besides spaghetti and macaroni try *tagliatelle* or the larger *fettuccine* ribbon noodles; baked *lasagne* with layers of pasta, meat sauce, and béchamel; rolled *cannelloni;* and *ravioli*. From there, you launch into the lusty poetry of *tortellini* and *cappelletti* (variations on *ravioli*), or curved *linguine*, flat *pappardelle*, quill-shaped *penne,* and corrugated *rigatoni*. Furthermore, there are almost as many sauces for pasta. The most famous, of course, is *bolognese*, or *ragù*. The tastiest version boasts not only minced beef, tomato purée, and onions but chopped chicken livers, ham, carrots, celery, white wine, and nutmeg. Other popular sauces are the simple *pomodoro* (tomato, garlic, and basil), *aglio e olio* (garlic, olive oil, and chili peppers), *carbonara* (chopped bacon and eggs), *matriciana* (salt pork and tomato), *pesto* (basil and garlic ground in olive oil with pine nuts and parmesan cheese), and *vongole* (clams).

Pizza: Another Italian invention familiar around the world, pizza is in reality a much more elaborate affair than you may be used to; the classic is *margherita* named for an Italian queen, with tomato sauce and melted mozzarella. Toppings can include any of the following: tomato, ham, anchovies, cheese, mushrooms, peppers, artichoke hearts, zucchini flowers, potatoes, egg, clams, tuna fish, garlic, or any other ingredient that takes the cook's fancy. A number of restaurants that grew too expensive during the years of the bribery scandals have converted to pizzerias. Note that in the summer pizzerias are not usually open for lunch because of the summer heat and the heat of their ovens.

Meat: A normal steak served to one person in a US restaurant would feed a family of four in Italy. Portions are smaller, since Italians eat several courses. *Vitello* (veal) is very popular; Rome's specialty is *saltimbocca* (literally "jump in the mouth"), a veal roll with ham, sage, and Marsala wine. Try the *cotoletta* (pan-fried cutlet in breadcrumbs), or the *scaloppine al limone* (with lemon). *Osso buco* is a delicious dish of stewed veal shin-bone in butter, with tomatoes, onions, finely-chopped lemon rind, and marrow.

Manzo (beef), *maiale* (pork), and *agnello* (lamb) are most often served in straightforward style: charcoal-grilled or *al forno* (roasted). *Bistecca alla fiorentina* (grilled Florentine T-bone), the emperor of all steaks, costs a royal ransom, but you should try it once.

Romans also claim the best *capretto* (roast kid); *porchetta* (suckling pig, roasted whole on a spit); and *abbacchio* (spring lamb), flavoured with garlic, sage, and rosemary, and seasoned just before serving with anchovy paste.

People-watch the Roman way — from a tableside at an outdoor café.

The most common chicken dishes are *pollo alla diavola* (grilled) or *petti di pollo alla bolognese* (filleted with ham and cheese). **Fish:** It's prepared in a simple way — grilled, steamed or fried. You should look out for *spigola* (sea bass), *triglia* (red mullet), *pesce spada* (swordfish), and *coda di rospo* (angler fish). The *fritto misto* is mixed fried seafood, mostly shrimp and octopus. **Vegetables:** These are ordered separately, as they do not automatically come with the main course. What is available will depend on the season, but you are most likely to find *spinaci* (spinach), *cicoria* (chicory), *fagiolini* (string beans in butter and garlic), *piselli* (peas), and *zucchini*.

Aristocrats among cooked vegetables are the *funghi porcini* (big boletus mushrooms), which sometimes come stuffed (*ripieni*) with bacon, garlic, parsley, and cheese. The white truffle is an autumn delicacy, and very expensive. Try also *peperonata* (red peppers stewed with tomatoes) or *melanzane* (eggplant) sometimes stuffed with anchovies, olives, and capers. The Jewish ghetto originated *carciofi alla giudea* (whole artichokes, crisply fried: stem, heart, leaves, and all). **Cheese:** The famous *parmigiano* (Parmesan), far better than the exported product, is eaten separately, not just grated over soup or pasta. Try also the blue *gorgonzola*, creamy *fontina*, pungent cow's milk *taleggio,* or ewe's milk *pecori-*

Do Drink the Water

Rome's drinking water, not least from its outdoor fountains, is famous for its flavor and is perfectly safe. Nonetheless, with meals it is customary to drink bottled mineral water. If tap water is not drinkable it will usually carry a sign saying *acqua non potabile*.

I'd like a bottle of mineral water.	**Vorrei una bottiglia di acqua minerale.**
carbonated/still	**gassata/naturale**

no. Ricotta can be sweetened with sugar and cinnamon for a delicious dessert.

Dessert: This often means *gelato*, the creamiest ice cream in the world. It's usually better in an ice-cream parlour (*gelateria*) than in the average *trattoria*. *Zuppa inglese* (literally "English soup"), the Italian version of trifle, can be anything from an extremely thick and sumptuous mixture of fruit, cream, cake, and Marsala to a disappointing sickly slice of cake. You may prefer the coffee-flavored trifle or *tiramisù* (literally "pick me up"). *Zabaglione* (whipped egg yolks, sugar, and Marsala) should be served warm or sent back. Fresh fruit can be a succulent alternative: *fragole* (strawberries), served with whipped cream or lemon; *uva* (grapes); and *albicocche* (apricots).

Drinks

Wine: Most restaurants offer the open wine of the house, red or white, in 1/4-litre, 1/2-litre, or 1-litre carafes, as well as a good selection of bottled vintages. Rome's "local" wine comes from the surrounding province of Lazio. The whites from the Alban Hills, called *Castelli Romani*, are light and pleasant and can be sweet or dry. The most famous is Frascati. From farther afield, the Chiantis of Tuscany are available everywhere; as are the velvety Valpolicella from the Veneto and Piedmont's full-bodied Barolo. Look out for the unusual Est! Est! Est! from Montefiascone on Lake Bolsena.

Italian beer: Beer is increasing in popularity, but is not as strong as north European brands.

Apéritif: Bitters such as Campari and Punt e Mes are refreshing with soda and lemon. For after-dinner drinks, try the anise-flavoured *sambuca* with a *mosca,* (coffee bean; literally a fly) swimming in it, or *grappa,* distilled from grapes, or the latest *moda*, icy *limoncello*, made from lemons.

To Help You Order...

Waiters are called *cameriere* (men) or *cameriera* (women).

Do you have a set menu? **Avete un menù a prezzo fisso?**

I'd like a/an/some... **Vorrei...**

beer	**una birra**	pepper	**del pepe**
bread	**del pane**	potatoes	**delle patate**
butter	**del burro**	salad	**un'insalata**
coffee	**un caffè**	salt	**del sale**
cream	**della panna**	soup	**una minestra**
fish	**del pesce**	sugar	**dello zucchero**
fruit	**della frutta**	tea	**un tè**
ice-cream	**un gelato**	(mineral)	**dell'acqua**
meat	**della carne**	water	**(minerale)**
milk	**del latte**	wine	**del vino**

...and Read the Menu

aglio	garlic	**manzo**	beef
agnello	lamb	**mela**	apple
albicocche	apricots	**melanzane**	eggplant
aragosta	lobster	**merluzzo**	cod
arancia	orange	**ostriche**	oysters
bistecca	beefsteak	**pesca**	peach
braciola	chop	**piselli**	peas
calamari	squid	**pollo**	chicken
carciofi	artichokes	**pomodori**	tomatoes
cipolle	onions	**prosciutto**	ham
crostacei	shellfish	**rognoni**	kidneys
fegato	liver	**tacchino**	turkey
formaggio	cheese	**uovo**	egg
frutti di mare	seafood	**uvas**	grapes
funghi	mushrooms	**verdure**	vegetables
lamponi	raspberries	**vitello**	veal
maiale	pork	**vongole**	clams

HANDY TRAVEL TIPS

An A–Z Summary of Practical Information

A

ACCOMMODATIONS

Rome's array of lodgings ranges from the spartan to the palatial. Hotels (*alberghi*) are classified in five categories, graded from 1 to 5 stars, based on the amenities and comfort they offer. (The Italian Tourist Board no longer uses the term *pensione* in its classifications; these family-style boarding houses are now graded as hotels, usually 1 or 2 stars.) Some religious institutions also take guests at reasonable rates.

High season is considered Easter through October when booking ahead is important, but for the rest of the year you can normally find accommodation in your preferred category without difficulty, although decent inexpensive hotels are usually booked far ahead. The Rome Tourist Board (EPT) has up-to-date hotel information (see Tourist Information, page 123). The EPT also has information offices at the (Roma-Nord) Salaria service area on the A1 *autostrada* (motorway) and at the (Roma-Sud) Frascati service area on the A2 *autostrada*. Alternatively, H.R. Hotel Reservation offers a telematic reservation service free of charge (Tel. 06-6991000) and has desks at Fiumicino airport and Termini railway station.

All room rates quoted should include taxes and service. The more expensive hotels have air-conditioning; in lower category hotels, if available, it sometimes costs extra.

Rome has several "daytime" hotels, one of them at Termini station; they provide bathrooms and luggage storage facilities for those with hours to kill between trains. At Fiumicino, the Hilton Rome Airport, on Via Arturo Ferrarin, is near the main terminal (Tel. 06-65258, fax 06-65256525).

I'd like a single/double room with bath/shower.	**Vorrei una camera singola/ doppia con bagno/doccia**

What's the rate per night?   **Qual è il prezzo per notte?**

AIRPORTS *(Aeroporti)*

Rome is served by two airports, Leonardo da Vinci, more common-
ly referred to as **Fiumicino**, 30 km (18 miles) southwest of the city,
and **Ciampino**, 15 km (9 miles) southeast of the city on the Via
Appia Nuova. Fiumicino handles mainly scheduled air traffic;
Ciampino is used by most charter companies. Fiumicino has two
terminals (domestic and international), a five-minute walk apart.

Fiumicino is connected by train to Termini railway station (service
is available approximately every half hour; journey 30 minutes; first
and last departures 7:37am and 10:37pm), and to Tiburtina railway
station (service every 15 minutes via Trastevere, Ostiense stations;
journey 40 minutes; first and last departures 5:57am and 11:27pm). A
late night COTRAL bus runs between Fiumicino and Tiburtina station during the hours when there is no train service. Termini is connected to metro lines A and B, and to buses which take you all over
the city; Tiburtina is linked to the city center by a variety of buses.

Information: Fiumicino, Tel. 06-65951; Ciampino, Tel. 06-
794941; Termini, Tel. 1478-88088

B

BUDGETING FOR YOUR TRIP

To give you an idea of what to expect, here's a list of approximate
prices in *lire* (L).

Airport transfer: Train from Fiumicino Airport to Roma Termini
L16,000; to Tiburtina railway station L8,000. Bus from Ciampino
Airport to Anagnina Metro station L1,500. Taxi from Fiumicino to
city center, minimum L70,000.

Buses, metro, and trains (urban network): Standard fare (*biglietto*) L1,500 (valid for 75 minutes); day ticket (BIG or *biglietto inte-*

Rome

grato giornaliero) L6,000; weekly ticket (CIF or *carta integrato settimanale*) L24,000.

Car rental: Unless you've made your reservations from home for lower rates, expect to pay: Fiat Punto L220,000 per day with unlimited mileage, L518,000 per week with max 150km(95 miles)/day. Alfa 156 L410,000 per day with unlimited mileage, L763,000 per week with max 150km(95 miles)/day.

Entertainment: Cinema L13,000, discotheque (entry and first drink) L30,000–40,000, outdoor opera L30,000–90,000.

Hotels: (double room with bath, including tax and service): 5-star L700,000–850,000, 4-star L360,000–600,000, 3-star L180,000–260,000, 2-star L90,000–140,000, 1-star L50,000–90,000.

Meals and drinks: Continental breakfast L15,000, lunch/dinner in fairly good establishment L35,000–50,000, coffee served at a table L4,000–6,000, served at the bar L900–1,500. Also at the bar: bottle of beer L3,000, soft drinks L3,000–5,000, aperitif L6,000 and up.

Museums: L8,000–15,000.

Taxis: Meter starts at L4,500, with L600 for each successive minute or L1,300 for each kilometer. Surcharge for night-time, holidays, Sundays, and each piece of luggage L5,000–2,000.

C

CAMPING *(Campeggio)*
Rome and the surrounding countryside have some 20 official campsites, most equipped with electricity, water, and toilet facilities. They are listed in the telephone directory under "Campeggio-Ostelli-Villaggi Turistici," or contact Roma Camping, Via Aurelia 831; Tel. 06-6623018. You can also contact the Tourist Office for a compre-

hensive list of sites and rates. Rates are usually around L14,500 per person per night; caravan (trailer) or camper L13,000; tent L7,000; car L7,000; motorbike L4,000.

The Touring Club Italiano (TCI) and the Automobile Club d'Italia (ACI) also publish lists of campsites and tourist villages, available at bookstores or the Tourist Office. You are strongly advised to stick to the official sites. If you enter Italy with a caravan (trailer), you're expected to show an inventory (with two copies) of the material and equipment in the caravan, e.g., dishes, linen, etc.

Is there a campsite near here?	**C'è un campeggio qui vicino?**
We have a tent/caravan (trailer).	**Abbiamo la tenda/la roulotte**.

CAR RENTAL/HIRE (*Autonoleggio*)

The major car-hire firms, Hertz, Avis, Budget, and Maggiore, have offices at the airports as well as in the city, listed in the telephone directory. To rent a car you must be at least 21 years of age and have held a valid driver's license for at least a year. Mandatory third-party insurance is included in the rates. A car rented in one Italian city can be dropped off in another, usually for an added cost. Note that hiring a car is expensive in Italy (see Budgeting for Your Trip, page 101). It is almost always cheaper and more convenient to book in advance from home, or as part of a fly-drive package. Before you leave home, review what is covered and what is not with your home-based office, and check the coverage offered by your credit card.

I'd like to rent a car	**Vorrei noleggiare una macchina**
for one day	**per un giorno**
for one week	**per una settimana**

CLIMATE

From June to mid-September, temperatures in Rome range from warm to very hot — it is not unusual to find 90° temperatures in the

Rome

afternoon in July and August. Winters are cool, often cold, and at times rainy, with occasional snow, but there are many sunny days. Spring and autumn are mild.

		J	F	M	A	M	J	J	A	S	O	N	D
Max*	°F	52	55	59	66	74	82	87	86	79	71	61	55
	°C	11	13	15	19	23	28	31	30	26	22	16	13
Min*	°F	40	42	45	50	56	63	67	67	62	55	49	44
	°C	4	5	7	10	12	17	19	19	18	13	9	6

CONSULATES *(Consolati)*

Contact the offices of your diplomatic representative if you lose your passport or run into serious trouble. Consulates can also provide lists of English-speaking doctors, lawyers, and interpreters.

Australia: Via Alessandria 215; Tel. 06-852721.

Canada: Via G.B. dei Rossi 27; Tel. 06-445981.

Ireland: P.zza Campitelli 3; Tel. 06-6979121.

New Zealand: Via Zara 28; Tel. 06-4417171.

South Africa: Via Tanaro 14; Tel. 06-852541.

UK: Via XX Settembre 80/a; Tel. 06-48903708/77.

US: Via Vittorio Veneto 121; Tel. 06-46741.

CRIME AND SAFETY

Unfortunately pickpockets and purse-snatchers are not uncommon in Rome, and easy-to-spot tourists are a favorite target. Carry with you only what is absolutely necessary; leave passports, airline tickets, and all but one credit card in the hotel safe. Use a money belt or carry your valuables in an inside pocket. For women, a small purse worn bandolier-style or even under a coat in winter, is best. Be especially careful on crowded public transport (beware the notorious tourist-filled bus 64 from Termini station to the Vatican) and in deserted streets. Groups of begging children holding signs and trying to distract you, are very adept pickpockets (they often linger around Termini, the Forum, or crowded shopping streets.)

Never leave anything in a parked car. Always lock it, with the glove compartment open, to discourage prospective thieves. When possible, park in a garage or attended parking area.

Make photocopies of your airline tickets, driving license, passport, and other vital documents to facilitate reporting any theft and obtaining replacements. Report thefts to the police, so that you have a statement to file with your insurance claim. The central police station is at: Questura Centrale, Via San Vitale 15; Tel. 06-4686.

I want to report a theft.   **Voglio denunciare un furto**.

My wallet/handbag/passport/ **Mi hanno rubato il portafoglio/**
ticket has been stolen.   **la borsa/il passaporto/il biglietto**.

CUSTOMS AND ENTRY REQUIREMENTS

For a stay of up to three months, a valid passport is sufficient for citizens of Australia, Canada, New Zealand, and the United States. Visitors from Ireland, the United Kingdom, and other EU countries need only an identity card to enter Italy. Tourists from South Africa must have a visa.

Here are some of the main items you can take into Italy duty-free and, when returning home, back to your own country:

	Cigarettes		Cigars		Tobacco	Spirits		Wine
Italy*	200	or	50	or	250*g*	2*l*	and	2*l*
Australia	200	or	250*g*	or	250*g*	1*l*	or	1*l*
Canada	200	and	50	and	400*g*	1.1*l*	or	1.1*l*
Ireland	200	or	50	or	250*g*	1*l*	and	2*l*
N. Zealand	200	or	50	or	250*g*	1.1*l*	and	4.5*l*

Rome

S. Africa	400	and	50	and	250*g*		1*l*	and	2*l*	
UK	400	or	100	or	500*g*		1*l*	and	2*l*	
US	100	and	50	and	**		1*l*	or	1*l*	
Within the EU**	800	and	200	and	1*kg*		10*l*	and	90*l*	

* These amounts apply to residents outside the EU or from duty-free shops within EU countries.

** Guidelines for non duty-free within the EU. For EU duty-free allowances see * above.

Currency restrictions: As a foreign tourist, you may import unlimited amounts in local or other currencies, but to take more than L20,000,000 or the equivalent in foreign money out again, you must fill in a V2 declaration form at the border when you arrive.

I've nothing to declare.   **Non ho nulla da dichiarare**.

D

DISABLED VISITORS
Cobblestone streets and steep hills are just two of the problems facing travelers with disabilities in Rome. There are lavatories for disabled people at both the main airports, at Stazione Termini, and Piazza San Pietro. St. Peter's and the Vatican Museums are wheelchair-accessible, but most of the city's other major museums and galleries are not. Up-to-date information on access to museums and monuments is provided by the Rome Tourist Board's free leaflet, *Musei e Monumenti di Roma*.

DRIVING
Entering Italy: To bring your car into Italy, you will need:

* an international driving license or valid national one

* car registration papers

- green insurance card (an extension to your regular insurance, making your policy valid for Italy)

- a red warning triangle in case of breakdown

- national identity sticker for your car.

Drivers of cars that are not their own must have the owner's written permission. Before leaving home, check with your automobile association about the latest status of gas coupons (these give tourists access to cheaper fuel) in Italy, as their availability is constantly changing.

patente	driving license
libretto di circolazione	car registration papers
carta verde	green card

Rules and regulations: Seat belts are compulsory. Drive on the right, pass on the left. Traffic on major roads has right of way over that entering from side roads, but this is frequently ignored, so be very careful. At intersections of roads of similar importance, the car on the right theoretically has the right of way. When passing other vehicles, or remaining in the left-hand (passing) lane, keep your directional indicator flashing.

Speed limits on the *autostrade* (toll highways) are 130 km/h (80 mph); on other roads the limit is 90 km/h (55 mph). The limit in built-up areas is generally 60 km/h (37 mph). The traffic police (*polizia stradale*) patrol the highways and byways on motorcycles or in Alfa Romeos, usually light blue. Speeding fines often have to be paid on the spot — ask for a receipt (*ricevuta*). All cities and many towns and villages have signs posted at the outskirts indicating the telephone number of the local traffic police or *carabinieri*. The headquarters in Rome are at Viale Romania 45; Tel. 06-80981.

Rome

Are we on the right road for...?	**Siamo sulla strada giusta per...?**

Driving in Rome: Only the most intrepid motorist stays cool in the face of the Romans' hair-raising driving habits. However, Roman drivers are not reckless — simply attuned to a different concept of driving. If you observe the following ground rules and venture with prudence into the urban traffic whirlpool, you stand a good chance of coming out unscathed.

Check to the right and left and your rearview mirror all the time; don't take priority for granted with green lights and pedestrian crossings. To progress in a traffic jam, inch gently but confidently forward into the snarl-up. Being too polite is tantamount to abdicating your rights as a motorist. Be careful of scooters suddenly passing you on the right.

In the city center between the river, Piazza del Popolo, Piazza di Spagna, and Piazza Venezia, a traffic-free *zona blu* operates Monday–Friday 6:30am–6pm, and Saturday 2pm–6pm. Exceptions are taxis, buses, and cars with special permits.

If you need help: Call boxes are located at regular intervals on the *autostrade* in case of breakdowns or other emergencies. You can dial **116** for the English-speaking operators of **ACI**'s (Automobile Club of Italy's) breakdown service. ACI temporary membership can be arranged at main border crossings.

I've had a breakdown.	**Ho avuto un guasto.**
There's been an accident.	**C'è stato un incidente.**

Fuel: Service stations abound in Italy, usually with at least one mechanic on duty. Most stations close on Sunday, and on other days 2:30–3pm, but many have self-service pumps available during closing hours. Stations along the *autostrade* are open 24 hours a day. Fuel (*benzina*) is sold at government-set prices and comes in super (98–100 octane), lead-free (95-octane), normal (86–88 octane), and diesel (also called *gasolio*). For unleaded fuel, look for the pumps with green labels marked *senza piombo* or the abbreviation SP.

Fill the tank, please.	**Per favore, faccia il pieno.**
super/normal	**super/normale**
unleaded	**senza piombo**
diesel	**gasolio**
Check the oil/tires/battery.	**Controlli l'olio/i pneumatici/ la batteria.**

Parking: Parking is one of Rome's greatest challenges. Your wisest course is to find a legal parking space for the duration of your stay and walk or use public transportation. Paid parking areas are designated by blue lines. Buy a ticket from one of the frequently-spaced coin-accepting meters: cost is L2,000 per hour, available in increments of 15 minutes. On the meter-issued ticket, mark the time of your arrival, and leave it inside the windshield (if you overstay your time, you'll be ticketed). If you park in a tow-away zone, you will pay a heavy fine and spend precious time reclaiming your car. For towed away cars, contact the *vigili urbani* (municipal police) central headquarters at Via Consolazione 4; Tel. 06-67691. The Rome branch of ACI has various car parks in the center: e.g., Piazza del Popolo, Via Barberini. There are also private car parks; try Parking Ludovisi at Via Ludovisi; Tel. 06-4740632; open 5:30am–1:30am; or (the largest, always open) at Villa Borghese, entrance on Viale del Muro Torto.

Where's the nearest car park?	**Dov'è il parcheggio più vicino?**
Can I park here?	**Posso parcheggiare qui?**

Rome

Road signs: Most road signs employed in Italy are international pictographs, but here are some written ones you may come across:

Accendere le luci	Use headlights
Deviazione	Detour
Divieto di sorpasso	No passing
Divieto di sosta	No stopping
Lavori in corso	Road work
Passaggio a livello	Level crossing
Pericolo	Danger
Rallentare	Slow down
Senso unico	One-way street
Senso vietato/Vietato l'ingresso	No entry
Zona pedonale	Pedestrian zone

E

ELECTRICITY
Electric current is 220 volts, 50 Hz AC. Bring a multiple adapter plug (*una presa multipla*), or buy one as required.

EMERGENCIES
In an emergency you can phone the following numbers all over Italy 24 hours a day: Emergency services (ambulance, fire, police) **118**; *Carabinieri* (for urgent police action): **112**; Fire: **115**; Road assistance (ACI): **116**.

Careful!	**Attenzione!**
Help!	**Aiuto!**
Stop thief!	**Al ladro!**

G

GETTING THERE

A reliable travel agent will have full details of all the latest flight possibilities, fares, and regulations, or do your own search on the Internet (see page 124).

By Air: Rome's Fiumicino (Leonardo da Vinci) Airport is linked by frequent direct service to cities in Europe, North America, the Middle East, and Africa. Average flying times are: New York–Rome 8 hours; Los Angeles–Rome 13 hours; London–Rome 2½ hours; Sydney–Rome 26 hours.

By Car: Cross-Channel car ferries link the UK with France, Belgium, and Holland. Once on the continent, you can put your car on a train to Milan (starting points include Boulogne, Paris, and Cologne). Alternatively, you can drive from the Channel coast to Rome without leaving a motorway. The main north-south (Milan–Florence–Reggio di Calabria) and east-west (L'Aquila–Civitavecchia) motorways connect with Rome via a huge ring motorway (*grande raccordo anulare*).

By Rail: InterRail cards are valid in Italy, as is the **Eurailpass** for non-European residents (purchase yours before you leave home). Within Italy, you can obtain an **Italian Tourist Ticket** (*Biglietto Turistico di Libera Circolazione*) for unlimited first- or second-class rail travel for 8, 15, 21, or 30 days. For intended travel within Italy, a First Class pass for L40,000L (valid 6 months from time of first use) gives you a 30% discount on all first class tickets. For L40,000 (and valid one year) the *Carta Argento* entitles those who can prove they are over 60 to a 30% discount.

The **Freedom Pass** offers travel on any 3, 5, or 10 days within one month in several European countries. Contact the International Rail Centre, Victoria Station, London SW1Y 1JY (Tel. 0171 834 2345).

The **Kilometric Ticket** (*Biglietto Chilometrico*) can be used by up to five people and is valid for 20 trips or 3,000 km (1,860 miles), first or second class, over a period of two months.

GUIDES AND TOURS

Most hotels in Rome can arrange for multilingual guides or interpreters. At many museums and sites, taped tour commentaries can be rented. The **Italian Tourist Agency (CIT)**, Piazza della Repubblica 68 (Tel. 06-47941), and many private firms offer guided bus tours of all the major sites, plus excursions to other points of interest. Often tourists are picked up and dropped off at their hotels. A private all-purpose travel operation, **Enjoy Rome** (Tel. 06-445-1843; <www.enjoy-rome.it>) offers inexpensive walking tours of Rome daily.

Rome's municipal bus company, **ATAC**, provides an inexpensive 3-hour sightseeing tour which takes in many of the major sites. Guided bus tours on ATAC bus 110 depart every half hour, 10am–6pm, from Piazza dei Cinquecento, in front of the Termini train station (Tel. 06-46952252); tickets (L15,000) are available from the ATAC information booth located in the square. Another cheap tour can be taken on the regularly scheduled local electric minibus 119, whose route circles the historic center (ticket L1,500); pick it up in the Piazza del Popolo near the corner of Via del Corso. There is no guide nor taped commentary.

H

HEALTH AND MEDICAL CARE

If your health insurance policy does not cover you while abroad (note that Medicare does not have coverage outside the US), take out a short-term policy before leaving home. Visitors from EU countries carrying the E111 form, available from their local post offices, are entitled to emergency medical and hospital treatment under the Italian social security system.

If you need medical care, ask your hotel receptionist to help you find a doctor (or dentist) who speaks English. The US and British consulates (see page 104) have lists of English-speaking doctors. Local Health Units of the Italian National Health Service are listed in the phone directory under *Unità Sanitaria Locale*. The first-aid (*pronto soccorso,* or "Emergency Room") section of hospitals handles medical emergencies.

Pharmacies: The Italian *farmacia* is open during shopping hours (see page 117). Usually one operates at night and at weekends for each district on a rotating basis. Some are open daily 24 hours, like the Farmacia della Stazione in the Termini train station, Piazza dei Cinquecento 49 (Tel. 06-4880019). Bring an adequate supply of any prescribed medication from home.

I need a doctor/a dentist.	**Ho bisogno di un medico/ dentista.**
Where's the nearest (all-night) chemist?	**Dov'è la farmacia (di turno) più vicina?**

HOLIDAYS *(Festa)*

Banks, government offices, and most shops and museums close on public holidays. When a major holiday falls on a Thursday or a Tuesday, Italians may make a *ponte* (bridge) to the weekend, meaning that Friday or Monday is taken off as well. The most important holidays are:

1 January	*Capodanno*	New Year's Day
6 January	*Epifania*	Epiphany
25 April	*Festa della Liberazione*	Liberation Day
1 May	*Primo Maggio*	May Day
15 August	*Ferragosto*	Feast of the Assumption
1 November	*Ognissanti*	All Saints' Day

Rome

8 December	*L'Immacolata Concezione*	Immaculate Conception
25 December	*Natale*	Christmas Day
26 December	*Santo Stefano*	St. Stephen's Day
Moveable date:	*Lunedì di Pasqua*	Easter Monday

In addition, Rome has a local holiday on June 29, the *Festa di San Pietro e San Paolo*, the Feast of Saints Peter and Paul, the city's patron saints, when everything closes. Get to St. Peter's Square early if you want to be a part of this as there are huge crowds.

L

LANGUAGE

You will not find English spoken everywhere in Rome, as you do in some other European cities. However, Italians are usually very helpful and quick to understand what you want. Italians appreciate foreigners making an effort to speak their language, even if it's only a few words. In the major hotels and shops, staff usually speak some English.

Bear in mind the following tips on pronunciation:

"c" is pronounced like ch in change when it is followed by an "e" or an "i."

"ch" together sounds like the "c" in cat.

"g" followed by an "e" or an "i" is pronounced like "j" in jet.

"gh" together sounds like the "g" in gap.

"gl" together sounds like the "lli" in million.

"gn" is pronounced like "ni" in onion.

"sc"+ "i" is pronounced like "she."

M

MAPS *(Piante)*

The offices of the Rome Tourist Board give away basic street plans featuring a selection of local information. More detailed maps are on sale at newsstands. A useful bus network map is sold at the ATAC information booth in Piazza dei Cinquecento (near Termini Station).

MEDIA

A good selection of British and international English-language newspapers and magazines are on sale, although sometimes a day late, at the airport and main railway station, and at newsstands in the city center.

The supplement *Trovaroma*, published in the Thursday edition of the newspaper *La Repubblica*, provides comprehensive listings of cultural events in Rome. Other publications are the weekly English section of *Roma C'è*, "This Week in Rome," and the English-language *Time Out* (every two months). The monthly *Carnet di Roma*, published by the Rome Tourist Board in Italian, English, French, and German, also lists events, as does the English-language publication *Wanted in Rome* (every two weeks), available at most newsstands.

The RAI, Italy's state broadcasting system, has three TV channels. There are also various private national and local channels. Telemontecarlo offers CNN during the early morning hours (and many hotels offer it round the clock). During the tourist season, RAI radio broadcasts news in English at 10am Monday–Saturday and at 9:30am Sunday. Vatican Radio carries foreign-language religious news programs. British (BBC) American (VOA), and Canadian (CBC) stations are easily obtained on most radios.

Rome

Have you any English-language newspapers?	**Avete giornali in inglese?**

MONEY

Currency: Italy's monetary unit is the *lira* (plural *lire*, abbreviated L or Lit). Coins come in 50, 100, 200, 500, 1000 lira denominations; notes in L1,000, 2,000, 5,000, 10,000, 50,000, 100,000, and 500,000.

Currency exchange: Currency exchange offices (*cambio*) are usually open Monday–Friday, 9am–1:30pm and 2:30–6pm; some stay open Saturday. Both cambio and banks charge a commission. Banks generally offer higher exchange rates and lower commissions. Passports are sometimes required when changing money.

ATMs: Automatic currency-exchange machines (*bancomat*) are now operated by many banks. A growing number of independent (read: non-bank related) ATMs can also be found in the center of town. Check with your bank at home to make sure your PIN number is valid in Italy.

Credit cards and traveler's checks: Most hotels, shops, and restaurants take credit cards. If the card's sign is posted in the window they must accept it, although some will try to avoid doing so. Traveler's checks are accepted almost everywhere, but you will usually get better value if you exchange them at a bank. Passports are required when cashing traveler's checks. Eurochecks are fairly easily cashed in Italy.

I want to change some pounds/dollars.	**Desidero cambiare delle sterline/dei dollari.**
Do you accept traveler's checks?	**Accetta traveler's cheques?**
Can I pay with a credit card?	**Posso pagare con la carta di credito?**

O

OPEN HOURS

For some offices and tourist-oriented shops, the modern non-stop business day (called the *orario americano*) is gradually creeping in. But in true Mediterranean fashion, much of the city shuts or slows down after lunch.

Shops: Monday–Saturday; in summer 9am–1pm and 4–8pm, in winter 3:30–7:30pm. Half-day closing is usually Monday morning. However, some shops in the center are open 10am–7pm, and department stores are open all day. Food stores are open 7am–1:30pm and 5–7:30pm; in summer until 8pm. Except for supermarkets, there is a half-day closing, usually Thursday afternoon in winter, and Saturday afternoon in summer. Tourist shops stay open all day in high season, some remaining open on Sunday.

Post offices: Normally, Monday–Friday 8:30am–5:30pm, until noon Saturday. The main post office in Piazza San Silvestro stays open Saturday 9am–2pm and Sunday 9am–6pm.

Banks: Monday–Friday, 8:30am–1:30pm and again for an hour or so in the afternoon (usually 3–4pm).

Pharmacies: 8:30am–1pm and 4–8pm (though 24 hrs for some: see Health and Medical care).

Churches: are generally open daily from early morning to 12 or 12:30pm, and 4 or 5–7pm. They discourage Sunday morning visits except for those attending mass. St. Peter's and some of the larger basilicas remain open all day.

Museums and historic sites: These are usually open Tuesday–Sunday, 9am–2pm (if not earlier), and, in some cases, also 5–8pm.

These hours vary greatly: See page 123 or check with your hotel or the tourist office before setting off.

P

POLICE

The municipal police (*vigili urbani*), dressed in navy blue or summer white uniforms with white helmets, handle city traffic and other city police tasks. They are courteous and helpful to tourists, though they rarely speak a foreign language. Those who do act as interpreters display a special badge on their uniforms, which indicates the languages they speak.

The *carabinieri*, dressed in dark blue uniforms with a red stripe down the side of the trousers, deal with theft, more serious crimes, demonstrations, and military affairs. The national, or state, police (*polizia di stato*) are distinguished by their navy blue jackets and light blue trousers, and handle other police and administrative matters. (Also see "Driving" on page 106). The all-purpose emergency number, 118, will get you police assistance.

Where's the nearest police station?	**Dov'è il più vicino posto di polizia?**

POST OFFICES (*Posta or Ufficio Postale*)

Post offices handle telegrams, mail, and money transfers. Look for the yellow sign with PT in black. Postage stamps are also sold at tobacco shops and at some hotel desks. Post boxes are red — the slot marked *Per la Città* is for local mail only, the one labelled *Altre Destinazioni* is for all other destinations. Mail to and from Rome can be slow. The Vatican post is more efficient; buy Vatican stamps near the Tourist Office in St. Peter's Square and use the post boxes there or anywhere in Rome.

There is a *poste restante* service (also called *fermo posta*) at the main post office in Piazza San Silvestro. Don't forget your passport for identification when you go to pick up mail. You will have to pay a small fee.

Telegrams (*telegramme*) can be sent to destinations inside and outside Italy, as can telex messages. Fax service is available, here or through most hotels.

I'd like a stamp for this letter/ postcard.	**Desidero un francobollo per questa lettera/cartolina.**

PUBLIC TRANSPORTATION

Metropolitana or *metrò* (underground/subway): Rome has two underground railway lines. Line A runs from Via Ottaviano near the Vatican southeast to Via Anagnina, stopping at more than 20 stations and passing close to many of Rome's popular tourist sights. The intersecting Line B runs from Rebibbia in the northeastern part of the city through Stazione Termini to EUR in the southwest. Some trains branch off at Magliana and go on to the coast, reaching Ostia Antica and Lido di Ostia. Metro stations are identified by a large red sign containing a white letter "M." Tickets are sold at newsstands and tobacco shops, or can be purchased from machines at the stations.

Buses (*autobus*): Rome's fleet of orange buses serves every corner of the city. Although crowded on certain routes and at rush hours, they are an inexpensive way of getting around. Each bus stop (*fermata*) indicates the buses stopping there, their routes, and frequency. Tickets for buses must be bought in advance from ATAC booths, some newsstands and tobacco shops, or automatic dispensers. Enter the bus by the rear doors and punch your ticket in a machine; exit by the middle doors; remember that you must ring before your stop.

A single ticket is valid for 75 minutes and can be used on as many buses as you wish, but only once on the metro or train. 24-hour tickets (BIG) let you travel as much as you like by train, bus, and metro. Weekly tickets (CIF) are sold at the ATAC (transport authority) information booth in Piazza dei Cinquecento, in front of Stazione Termini. Network maps are available from the ATAC booth and from newsstands. COTRAL (Tel. 06-5915551) operates bus services to the outskirts of Rome. Buses to the Roman hills (e.g., Albano, Frascati, Castelgandolfo) leave from the COTRAL station at the Anagnina metro station.

Where's the nearest bus stop/ underground (subway) station?	**Dov'è la fermata d'autobus/ la stazione della metropolitana più vicina?**
When's the next bus/train to...?	**Quando parte il prossimo autobus/treno per...?**
I'd like a ticket to	**Vorrei un biglietto per...**

Horse-drawn carriages (*carrozzelle*): A familiar sight in Rome for centuries, horse-drawn carriages now number only a few dozen. They can be found at many of the major tourist sites across the city, including the Pantheon, St. Peter's Square, the Spanish Steps, and the Colosseum. A complete tour around the center of the city will cost you around L150,000.

Taxis (*tassì or taxi*): Rome's licensed yellow and white taxis cannot be flagged, but must be found at taxi ranks (on all the major piazzas) or summoned by telephone (Tel. 06-3875 or 06-3570). When you phone for a taxi, you pay a surcharge. Extra fees are also charged for luggage, night, holiday, Sunday, or airport trips: by law, the rates are posted in four languages inside all taxis. A tip of at least 10 percent is customary. Beware of the non-metered unlicensed taxis (*abusivi*), which charge much more than the normal taxi rates; they're often found at the airport and train stations.

R

RELIGION

Roman Catholic mass is celebrated daily and several times on Sunday in Italian. A few churches have occasional services in English. Confessions are heard in English in St. Peter's, Santa Maria Maggiore, St. John Lateran, St. Paul's Outside the Walls, among others.

A number of non-Catholic denominations have congregations in Rome with services in English. These include Church of England at All Saints, Via del Babuino 153; American Episcopal at St. Paul's, Via Napoli 58; Scottish Presbyterian at St. Andrew's, Via XX Settembre 7; Methodist at Via Banco di S. Spirito 3. The Jewish Synagogue is at Lungotevere Cenci 9. The city's first mosque is in Via della Moschea.

T

TELEPHONE *(Telefono)*

Public phone booths are scattered at strategic locations throughout the city. Calls can also be made from bars and cafés, indicated by a yellow telephone sign showing a telephone dial and receiver. The main public telephone office, in the Palazzo delle Poste in Piazza San Silvestro, is open day and night.

Public pay phones require 100-, 200-, and 500-lire coins or phone cards *(scheda telefonica)*. To make a call from a pay phone, insert the coin or card (with the serrated corner torn off) and lift the receiver. The normal dialing tone is a series of long dash sounds. A dot-dot-dot series means the central computer is overloaded; hang up and try again.

From telephones labelled *Teleselezione* you can make direct international calls, but be sure to have a good supply of coins. Most telephones take international phone cards of L5,000 or L10,000, available from some bars, tobacco shops, Telecom Italia branches, post offices, and automatic dispensers.

Rome

International calls from hotels are heavily surcharged; it is advisable that you use an American calling card for overseas calls. To connect with local service when using a calling card, for AT&T dial 172-1011, for MCI Worldphone dial 172-1022, Sprint 172-1877.

For the local directory and other Italian enquiries, **12**; European international operator, **15**; International enquiries, **176**; Intercontinental operator, **170**; Intercontinental enquiries, **1790**. Direct dialling for Australia: 0061, Canada: 001, Ireland: 00353, South Africa: 0027, UK: 0044, USA.: 001.

Give me ... coins/phone card please.	**Per, favore, mi dia...monete/ una scheda telefonica.**
L5,000/L10,000	**cinquemila/diecimila lire.**
Can you get me this number in?	**Può passarmi questo numero a...?**

TIME ZONES

Italy follows Central European Time (GMT + 1). From the last Sunday in March to the last Sunday in September, clocks are put ahead one hour (GMT + 2).

Summer Time Chart:

New York	London	**Italy**	Jo'burg	Sydney
6am	11am	**noon**	noon	8pm

TIPPING

Though a service charge (*servizio*) is added to most restaurant bills, it is customary to leave an additional nominal tip of a few lira notes: Leave up to L5,000 if service is already included in the bill. It is also usual to give porters, doormen, garage attendants, and others a little something for their services. Give a hotel porter L3,000 per bag; a chamber-maid L5,000 per day; a lavatory attendant L1,000. Tip taxi drivers, hairdressers/barbers, and tour guides 10 percent.

TOILETS

Most museums and art galleries have public toilets. Bars, restaurants, cafés, department stores, airports, railway stations, and car parks all have facilities. Carry your own tissues.

Toilets may be labeled with a symbol of a man or a woman or the initials W.C. Sometimes labels will be in Italian, but beware: *Uomini* is for men, *Donne* for women; however, *Signori* with a final "i" is for men, but *Signore* with a final "e" means women. Some facilities are unisex.

TOURIST INFORMATION

The **Italian National Tourist Office** (*Ente Nazionale Italiano per il Turismo*, abbreviated ENIT) is represented in Italy and abroad. They publish detailed brochures with up-to-date information on accommodation, means of transport, general tips, and useful addresses to tourists.

Australia and New Zealand: c/o Italian Government Tourist Office, Lions Building, 1-1-2 Moto Akasaka, Minato Ku, Tokyo 107; Tel. (03) 3478 2051.

Canada: Italian Government Travel Office, Suite 1914, 1 Place Ville-Marie, Montreal, Quebec, H3B 3M9; Tel. (514) 866 7667.

Ireland: Italian State Tourist Office, 47 Merrion Square, Dublin 2; Tel. (01) 766 397.

South Africa: Italian State Tourist Office, P.O. Box 6507, Johannesburg 2000.

UK: Italian State Tourist Office, 1 Princes Street, London W1R 6AY; Tel. (0171) 408 1254.

US: Italian Government Travel Office, Suite 1565, 630 Fifth Ave, New York, NY 10111, Tel. (212) 245 4822; Italian Government Travel Office, Suite 1046, 401 North Michigan Ave, Suite 3030,

Rome

Chicago, IL 60611, Tel. (312) 644 0996; Italian Government Travel Office, Suite 550, 12400 Wilshire Blvd, Los Angeles CA 90025, Tel. (310) 820 0098.

The Tourist Office's headquarters in **Rome** are at Via Parigi 5 (Tourist Assistance, Tel. 06-48899253/55, fax 06-488-99228), open Monday–Friday 8:15am–7:15pm, and Saturday 8:15am–1:45pm. It operates kiosks at Stazione Termini and two at Fiumicino Airport (both international and domestic arrivals), open daily 8:15–7:15pm. A general tourist information Call Center (Tel. 06-36004399), with operators speaking Italian, English, French, Spanish and German will answer any and all questions regarding tourism in Rome (open daily 9am–7pm).

Launched in anticipation of the Jubilee 2000 are new tourist information points maintained by the Comune di Roma (look for bright green kiosks), open daily from 9am–6pm. There are information points at Castel Sant' Angelo–Piazza Pia (Tel. 06-68809707); Fori Imperiali–Piazza del Tempio della Pace (Tel. 06-69924307); Piazza delle Cinque Lune (Tel. 06-68809240); Piazza Sonnino (Tel. 06-58333457); San Giovanni in Laterano (Tel. 06-77203535); and Stazione Termini (Tel. 06-48906300; near the biglietteria/ticket booth area; open 9am-8pm).

Where's the tourist office?   **Dov'è l'ufficio turistico?**

WEB SITES

A number of web sites have been set up by different divisions of city and federal tourism entities: <www.entenaz.it.perturismo>; <www.enit.it>; <www.romaturismo.com>. Set up for the Jubilee 2000, but expected to stay in operation: <www.romagiubileo.it>. For an affordable airfare to Rome, try <www.travelocity.com> or <www.bestfares.com>.

There are also a growing number of **internet cafés** located in the center where you can check your e-mail and also have a coffee or drink. A central Internet Cafe is at Via Cavour 213 (Tel. 06-47823051) is open daily from 9am–1am.

WEIGHTS AND MEASURES

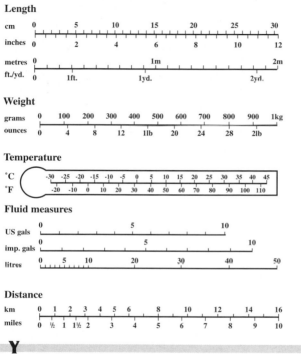

Length

Weight

Temperature

Fluid measures

Distance

Y

YOUTH HOSTELS *(Ostelli della Gioventù)*

Youth hostels are open to holders of membership cards issued by the International Youth Hostels Federation, or by the AIG *(Associazione Italiana Alberghi per la Gioventù)*

Recommended Hotels

Italian hotels are classified by the government from 1 to 5 stars according to the facilities they offer. However, the star rating does not give a guide to the character or location of the hotel. Prices don't always include breakfast so check this when you book. Inexpensive hotels are hard to find in Rome so book early.

As a basic guide we have used the symbols below to indicate high season prices for a double room with bath or shower, including service charge, tax, and VAT. Major credit cards include American Express (AE), Diners Club (DC), MasterCard (MC) and Visa (V).

$	below L200,000
$$	L200,000–400,000
$$$	above L400,000

Aldrovandi Palace *(Parioli)* **$$$** *Via Ulisse Aldovrandi, 15, 00197; Tel. 06-3223993; fax 06-3221435; web site <www. aldrovandi.com>.* This handsome hotel with Old World style and service is in a quiet, residential neighborhood, removed from downtown commotion. There are many amenities, particularly the pool, garden, and the Relais La Piscine restaurant. 143 rooms. Major credit cards.

Arenula *(Ghetto)* **$$** *Via Santa Maria dei Calderai 47, 00186; Tel. 06-6879454; fax 06-6896188; e-mail <hotelarenula@ flashnet.it>.* A comfortable and reasonably priced hotel, it's one of the very few in the heart of the Jewish Ghetto and is within striking distance of many major sites. 50 rooms. Major credit cards.

Atlante Star *(near St. Peter's)* **$$$** *Via Vitelleschi 34, 00193; Tel. 06-6879558/6873233; fax 06-6872300; e-mail <atlante.star@*

atlantehotels.com>. Among the attractions offered here is the spectacular 360-degree view of St. Peter's from its well-known and much respected roof-garden restaurant, Les Etoiles, and from many of the rooms. The rooms have a contemporary decor, and service is courteous, with lots of up-market attention to details. 60 rooms. Major credit cards.

Barrett *(near Largo Argentina)* **$** *Largo Torre Argentina 47, 00186; Tel. 06-6868481; fax 06-6892971.* Though extremely small, with only 15 rooms available, this hotel is very central and comfortable and remarkably good value for the money, only a five-minute stroll south of the Pantheon. No credit cards.

Brittania *(near Termini Station)* **$$** *Via Napoli 64, 00184; Tel. 06-4883153; fax 06-4882343; web site <www.italyhotel.com/roma/brittania>.* This comfortable hotel has a variety of amenities, such as television, mini-bar, room safe, and hair dryer, that are included in the moderate price. The convenient neighorhood is safe enough, but not very picturesque. 33 rooms. Major credit cards.

Carriage *(near Piazza di Spagna)* **$$** *Via delle Carrozze 36, 00187; Tel. 06-6990124; fax 06-6788279; e-mail <hotel.carriage@alfanet.it>.* A quiet hotel a stone's throw from the Spanish Steps, it sits amid the many shops and cafés. Rooms are stylishly furnished; the top-floor terrace is accessed by some of the larger and most in-demand rooms (request in advance when booking). 27 rooms. Major credit cards.

Cavalieri Hilton *(Monte Mario)* **$$$** *Via A. Cadlolo 101, 00136; Tel. 06-35091; fax 06-35092241; e-mail<sales_rome@hilton.com>.* Set amid 15 acres in a peaceful, but removed location (15 minutes from downtown), it has splendid views of the residential neighborhood of Monte Mario. Outdoor swimming pool, terrace, park, tennis. Excellent dining, indoors and alfresco. 359 rooms. Major credit cards.

Cesari *(near the Corso)* **$$** *Via di Pietra 89/a, 00186; Tel. 06-6792386; fax 06-6790882; e-mail <cesari@venere.it>.* A pleasant 18th-century hotel whose past guests — Stendhal, Mazzini, and Garibaldi — wouldn't recognize the 1990s modernization. The location is extremely central. 51 rooms. DC, MC only.

Columbus *(near St. Peter's)* **$$$** *Via della Conciliazione 33, 00193; Tel. 06-6865435; fax 06-6864874; e-mail <columbus@hotelcolumbus.net>.* This tastefully furnished hotel is in an impressive 15th-century palace built by Cardinal (and future Pope) Domenico della Rovere. There are original frescoes in the lobby and a fine restaurant. Its proximity to St. Peter's (3 blocks from St. Peter's Square) has made it a longtime favorite of visiting Vatican officials. 92 rooms. Major credit cards.

Condotti *(near Piazza di Spagna)* **$$** *Via Mario dei Fiori 37, 00187; Tel. 06-6794661; fax 06-6790457; web site <www.venere.it/roma/condotti>.* A quiet and comfortable hotel, it is in the very heart of Rome's most exclusive shopping district. Hotel pickings are slim for this price range in this tony pedestrian-only area. 16 rooms. Major credit cards.

Dei Borgognoni *(Corso/Via del Tritone)* **$$$** *Via del Bufalo 126, 00187; Tel. 06-69941505; fax 06-69941501; e-mail <hotel.borgognoni@flashnet.it>.* An elegant hotel offering excellent service, it's almost within splashing distance of the fabled Trevi Fountain and other important attractions. Some of the rooms have private gardens or terraces. 50 rooms. Major credit cards.

Eden *(near Via Veneto)* **$$$** *Via Ludovisi 49, 00187; Tel. 06-478121; fax 06-4821584; web site <www.hotel-eden.it>.* This recently renovated hilltop luxury hotel has excellent views of the city from the famous rooftop terrace bar and restaurant. It's halfway between the Spanish Steps and the Via Veneto. 119 rooms. Major credit cards.

Edera *(near Colosseum)* **$$** *Via Poliziano 75, 00184; Tel. 06-70453888/70453946; fax 06-70453769; e-mail <leonardi@travel. it>*. This is a quiet, unpretentious hotel with a small garden. No restaurant. 53 rooms. Major credit cards.

Excelsior $$$ *Via Veneto 125, 00187; Tel. 06-47081; fax 06-4826205; web site <www.luxurycollection.com>*. The grand dame of the turn-of-the-century hotels was recently renovated and is extremely comfortable. It's adjacent to the US Embassy and thus a natural magnet for Americans and the Hollywood types who fill the sophisticated bar. 329 rooms. Major credit cards.

Fontana $$$ *Piazza di Trevi 96, 00187; Tel. 06-6786113; fax 06-6790024*. A comfortable hotel housed in a converted monastery, it has smallish rooms but many of them with priceless views of the Baroque wonder that is the Trevi Fountain. Those without a view can repair to the roof garden and terrace. 25 rooms. Major credit cards.

Forum *(near Piazza Venezia)* **$$$** *Via Tor dei Conti 25, 00184; Tel. 06-6792446; fax 06-6786479; e-mail <www.hotelforum.com>*. An elegantly furnished hotel that has a spectacular view of the Imperial Forums from its delightful roof-garden restaurant, a perfect spot for both lunch and dinner. The Colosseum is a short walk away. 81 rooms. Major credit cards.

Gerber *(Prati)* **$$** *Via degli Scipioni 241, 00192; Tel. 06-3216485; fax 06-3217048; e-mail <info@hotelgerber.it>*. This is a small hotel with simple rooms in a quiet neighborhood north of the Vatican. A garden and sun terrace add to the comforts provided. 27 rooms. Major credit cards.

Gregoriana *(above the Spanish Steps)* **$$** *Via Gregoriana 18, 00187; Tel. 06-6794269; fax 06-6784258.* In a particularly pleasant location at the top end of the Spanish Steps, this converted convent has distinctive Art-Deco style. Its pretty, comfortable rooms attract regular return guests, many in the fashion industry. 16 rooms. Major credit cards.

Hassler Villa Medici *(above the Spanish Steps)* **$$$** *Piazza Trinità dei Monti 6, 00187; Tel. 06-6993401, Reservations 69941607; fax 06-6789991; e-mail <hasslerroma@mclink.it>.* In a wonderful location overlooking the Spanish Steps and all of Rome, it has furnishings, house-proud service, and a spectacular rooftop bar and restaurant to match. A few choice suites have remarkable terraces for the absolute splurge. 100 rooms. Major credit cards.

Holiday Inn Crowne Plaza Minerva *(near the Pantheon)* **$$$** *Piazza della Minerva 69, 00186; Tel. 06-695201; fax 06-6794165; e-mail <minerva@pronet.it>.* An elegant 17th-century palazzo that has been a lodging place since Napoleonic times, and is now Rome's newest luxury hotel. Many of the tastefully decorated contemporary rooms overlook Bernini's Piazza Minerva. 134 rooms. Major credit cards.

D'Inghilterra *(Corso/Piazza di Spagna)* **$$$** *Via Bocca di Leone 21, 00187; Tel. 06-69981; fax 06-6798601; e-mail <reservation_hir@charminghotels.it>.* A perennial favorite sits amid the grid of top-of-the-line designer boutiques near the Spanish Steps. Antique furniture and a fine collection of Neapolitan gouaches preserve a distinct flavor of the past. Celebrity guests such as Ernest Hemingway, Mark Twain, and Henry James found it a gem. 105 rooms. Major credit cards.

Locarno (*near Piazza del Popolo*) **$$** *Via della Penna 22, 00186; Tel. 06-3610841/3216030; fax 06-3215249; e-mail <info@hotellocarno.com>*. A centrally located hotel with a charming vine-covered facade and a lobby in Art Nouveau style. There's a lovely small outdoor courtyard for breakfast, or take a two-block walk to the Piazza del Popolo for a sunny alternative. 38 rooms. Major credit cards.

Majestic $$$ *Via V. Veneto 50, 00187; Tel. 06-421441; fax 06-4880984; e-mail <hotel.majestic@flashnet.it>*. Tastefully refurbished in deluxe style, this hotel is a perfect blend of old and new. Every room is individually furnished and all bathrooms are in Carrara marble with Jacuzzi bathtubs. One of the old-time favorites of the Via Veneto since its 1950s golden days.100 rooms. Major credit cards.

Margutta (*near Piazza del Popolo*) **$** *Via Laurina 34, 00187; Tel. 06-3223674; fax 06-32200395.* A small but very centrally located hotel with eclectic decor, it attracts faithful return guests and offers reliable service with a smile. A few of the small rooms on the upper floor have their own terraces with views. 24 rooms. Major credit cards.

Mediterraneo (*near Termini Station*) **$$$** *Via Cavour 15, 00184; Tel. 06-4884051; fax 06-4744105; e-mail <hb@bettojahotels.it>*. This period piece from the 1930s is in solemn Classical style, with busts and statues, mosaics, and maps, all on the theme of the Mediterranean. There are wonderful views over the city from the terrace on the tenth floor. However, for these prices, a nicer location would be preferable. 266 rooms. Major credit cards.

Portoghesi (*near Piazza Navona*) **$$** *Via dei Portoghesi 1, 00186; Tel. 06-6864231; fax 06-6876976; e-mail <portoghesi@*

venere.it>. Beat the devoted regulars and book early at this popular, reasonably priced, small hotel in a picturesque corner of Rome's Centro Storico. Modern bathrooms, air conditioning, television, and telephones are in each of the 27 comfortable, carpeted rooms. MC only.

Quirinale *(near Piazza della Repubblica)* **$$$** *Via Nazionale 7, 00184; Tel. 06-4707; fax 06-4820099; e-mail <hotel.quirinale@ mclink.it>*. A large, efficiently run hotel, it's just next door to the Teatro dell'Opera, the main reason for its popularity. Garden, outdoor dining in summer. 205 rooms. Major credit cards.

Raphael *(near Piazza Navona)* **$$$** *Largo Febo 2, 00186; Tel. 06-682831; fax 06-6878993; e-mail <raphaelhotel.com>*. With a vine-draped facade, this intimate establishment is decorated with antiques in the lobby and in many of the comfortable rooms. There is both a restaurant and bar in the hotel, but they're easy to overlook with Rome's loveliest piazza five steps away. Views from the terrace garden are hard to forget. 69 rooms. Major credit cards.

Saint Regis Grand *(near Termini Station)* **$$$** *Via Vittorio Emanuele Orlando 3, 00185; Tel. 06-47091; fax 06-4747307; web site <www.luxurycollection.com>*. The Grand Hotel has a new name and a brand new look thanks to a complete redecoration as of 1999. Stop by if only for afternoon tea, a year round tradition, particularly in the winter. Better yet, check into one of Rome's most lavish guest rooms. 171 rooms. Major credit cards.

Scalinata di Spagna *(above Piazza di Spagna)* **$$$** *Piazza Trinità dei Monti 17, 00187; Tel. 06-6793006; fax 06-6840598*. The view over the city and down the Spanish Steps from this charming former-pensione-turned-up-market boutique hotel is fantastic. Rooms are modest for these rates, but always full nonetheless — location, location, location. 15 rooms. Major credit cards.

Senato *(near the Pantheon)* **$$$** *Piazza della Rotonda 73, 00186; Tel. 06-6793231; fax 06-69940297; e-mail <delsenato @italyhotel.com>.* This comfortable hotel is in the atmospheric heart of Rome's historical center. Some rooms have a view of the Pantheon, or you can alternate your evenings with those spent in the nearby Piazza Navona. 60 rooms. Major credit cards.

Sole *(near Campo dei Fiori)* **$** *Via del Biscione 76, 00186; Tel. 06-6879446; fax 06-6893787; e-mail <sole@italyhotel.com>.* One of the few budget-priced hotels left in town, this one has individually decorated rooms that vary greatly. But one comes here for the medieval neighborhood, alive from early morning at the Campo dei Fiori market until late evening, with shops and restaurants. 58 rooms. No credit cards.

Sole Al Pantheon *(near the Pantheon)* **$$$** *Piazza della Rotonda 63, 00186; Tel. 06-6780441; fax 06-69940689; e-mail <hotelsolealpantheon.com>.* An inn for 500 years, the recently refurbished boutique hotel retains all its charm while adding modern comforts and boasting an excellent location. Each of the 25 rooms is named after an illustrious guest of the distant past. Major credit cards.

Suisse *(near Piazza di Spagna)* **$$** *Via Gregoriana 56, 00187; Tel. 06-6783649; fax 06-6781258.* This is a comfortable, efficiently family-run third-floor hotel in a good location near the Spanish Steps and hotels quadruple these rates. No fuss, and very popular. 12 rooms. 50% of bill can be paid with DC, MC or V.

Recommended Restaurants

Authentic Roman cuisine has its basis in la *cucina povera*, the poor man's cooking. You will find these simple but delicious traditional dishes not only in most Roman *trattorie* but also in the most elegant and expensive of restaurants. By law the nominal charge for *pane e coperto* has been eliminated, but check before paying. Note that around the national holiday of *Ferragosto* (August 15) many restaurants close for two, three, sometimes four weeks, as Romans head out of town. Restaurants also close for a week or so sometime between Christmas and mid-January: it's best to call in advance during these periods.

Roman restaurants serve lunch from 12:30 to 3pm and dinner from 7 or 8pm to 11pm. Some offer late-night supper and are open until 1 or 2am.

The following symbols are designed to give you some idea of the price for a three-course meal with wine and service included:

$	below L 40,000
$$	L 40,000-70,000
$$$	above L 70,000

Agata e Romeo *(near Santa Maria Maggiore)* **$$$** *Via Carlo Alberto 45, 00184; Tel. 06-4466115; fax 06-4465842.* Lunch and dinner; closed Monday. This restaurant, managed by sommelier Romeo together with his talented wife Agata in the kitchen (and their daughter), is considered one of the best in Rome. Traditional dishes with a fresh twist, and desserts to die for include lemon mousse with raspberry sauce and chocolate fondant with orange sauce. Reservations a must. Major credit cards.

Alberto Ciarla *(Trastevere)* **$$$** *Piazza San Cosimato 40, 00153; Tel. 06-5818668; fax 06-5884377.* Dinner only; closed

Sunday. Recommended for elegant seafood and fish dishes, and worth a visit for the iced-fish display alone. Outdoor dining is available. Stroll about after dinner to take a look at this colorful neighborhood. Reservations recommended. Major credit cards.

Campana *(near Piazza Navona)* **$$** *Vicolo della Campana 18, 00186; Tel. 06-6867820.* Lunch and dinner; closed Monday. A popular, typically local *trattoria* since 1518, with all the old Italian favorites on the menu. Start with a selection from the antipasto table but save dessert for an after-dinner *gelato* in nearby Piazza Navona. Major credit cards.

Cannavota *(St. John Lateran)* **$$** *Piazza di San Giovanni in Laterano 20, 00184; Tel. 06-77205007.* Lunch and dinner; closed Wednesday. Charming, easy-going *trattoria* and one of the more popular haunts in the capital, offering hearty portions. Especially good for lasagna, risotto, and grilled fish. Major credit cards.

Charly's Sauciere *(St. John Lateran)* **$$** *Via San Giovanni in Laterano 270, 00184; Tel. 06-70495666.* Lunch and dinner; closed Saturday, Sunday, and Monday. The first French restaurant (the owners are Swiss) in Rome is still going strong. Cozy surroundings, graceful service and a favorite with Romans for its quality cuisine moderately priced. All the favorites topped by crepes suzettes. Major credit cards.

Checchino dal 1887 *(Testaccio)* **$$$** *Via Monte Testaccio 30, 00153; Tel. and fax 06-5743816.* Lunch and dinner; closed Sunday and Monday. An acclaimed first-rate *trattoria* serving a traditional cuisine based on the cheap cuts and offal from Testaccio's slaughterhouse. Tripe, brains, liver, sweetbreads, and intestines are loved by Romans but there's much else to keep more conservative palates happy. Reserve for dinner. Major credit cards.

Colline Emiliane *(near Piazza Barberini)* **$$** *Via degli Avignonesi 22, 00187; Tel. 06-4817538.* Lunch and dinner; closed Friday. Trattoria serving traditional and unforgettable specialities from Emilia-Romagna (and an unusual apple pie for dessert), the cradle of Italian cuisine. Delicious homemade pastas that change regularly are some of the best in Rome. Reservations recommended. No credit cards.

Il Convivio *(near Piazza Navona)* **$$$** *Vicolo dei Soldati 31, 00187; Tel. 06-8805950.* Dinner daily; closed for lunch Sunday and Monday. One of Rome's top restaurants, run by the three amiable Troiani brothers with Angelo in the kitchen. Imaginative un-Roman dishes such as pigeon breast in a cherry sauce with potato cake, or filet of sole with juniper sauce, spinach, and basmati rice. Excellent fairly-priced wine selection. Reservations a must. Major credit cards.

Corallo *(Piazza Navona)* **$** *Via del Corallo 10; Tel. 06-68307703.* Dinner only; closed Monday. This reliable neighborhood spot is known for good pizzas and a number of local dishes to fill out the menu. The *focaccia* (plain pizza) hot from the wood-burning oven is best sampled here. Major credit cards.

L'Eau Vive *(near Largo Argentina)* **$$** *Via Monterone 85, 00186; Tel. 06-68801095; fax 06-68802571.* Lunch and dinner; closed Sunday. Splendid French-colonial cuisine is served in a restaurant run by an order of lay missionaries and housed in a 16th-century papal palace. Non-smokers are rewarded with seating in a frescoed salon upstairs. Waitresses sing at 10pm. Reservations recommended. Major credit cards.

Hassler Roof Garden *(above Piazza di Spagna)* **$$$** *Piazza della Trinità dei Monti 6, 00187; Tel. 06-6792651.* Lunch and dinner, Sunday brunch; closed for dinner Sunday. A restaurant at the top of the Hassler Hotel with a one-of-a-kind panoramic view of the whole city. Excellent service and food, and a popular spot for a leisurely un-Roman Sunday brunch. Reservations recommended. Major credit cards.

Insalata Ricca I *(near Corso Vittorio Emanuele)* **$** *Largo dei Chiavari, 85; Tel. and fax 06-68803656; web site <www. linsalataricca.com>.* Lunch and dinner daily. Nice variety of fresh and savory entree-size salads are offered as well as a good selection of tasty pasta dishes. Claustrophobes won't enjoy the cozy seating, but non-smokers will. This is the original of what now numbers seven successful offspring. Major credit cards.

Il Matriciano *(Prati)* **$$** *Via dei Gracchi 55, 00192; Tel. 06-3212327; fax 06-3212327.* Lunch and dinner; closed Wednesday, November–May, Saturday, June–October. Situated close to the Vatican. Simple, country-style specialties served in a very comfortable atmosphere with outdoor umbrella tables. Reservations recommended. Major credit cards.

Monserrato *(near Piazza Navona)* **$$** *Via di Monserrato 96, 00187; Tel. 06-6873386.* Lunch and dinner; closed Monday. A good choice for moderately priced especially delicious food, with summer dining outdoors. Reliably good fish choices include *linguini* with large shrimp and green pepper, and grilled octopus. Meat-lovers will find good beef selections, too. Major credit cards.

Nino *(Piazza di Spagna)* **$$** *Via Borgogna 11; Tel. and fax 06-6795676.* Lunch and dinner; closed Sunday. Good traditional Tuscan food and Chianti wine selections have been long favored by the shop-owners and patrons of this chic neighborhood. Reasonably priced for such expensive real estate. MC, V.

Rome

Papà Giovanni *(near Piazza Navona)* **$$$** *Via dei Sediari 4; Tel. and fax 06-68804807; web site <www. papagiovannirome.com>.* Lunch and dinner; closed Sunday. One of the city's top restaurants, where simple and classical regional dishes are reinterpreted with style in a cozy and romantic ambience. The accent is on seasonal vegetables, fresh local market produce, and a good list of local wines. Major credit cards.

Paris in Trastevere *(Trastevere)* **$$** *Piazza di San Callisto 7/a, 00153; Tel. and fax 06-5815378.* Lunch daily; dinner Tuesday–Saturday. On offer at this delightful restaurant (not Parisian at all) are a charming Baroque dining room and a terrace for summertime dinners. A creative selection of both fish and meat entrees. Major credit cards.

La Pergola dell' Hotel Hilton *(Monte Mario)* **$$$** *Via Cadlolo 101, 00136; Tel. 06-35092211; fax 06-35092241.* Dinner only; closed Sunday and Monday. This elegant penthouse restaurant has a spectacular view overlooking the city and Roman hills and an acclaimed chef. Reservations essential. . Major credit cards.

Al Piccolo Arancio *(near Trevi Fountain)* **$** *Vicolo di Scanderberg 112; Tel. 06-6786139; fax 06-6780766.* Lunch and dinner; closed Monday. In a narrow alley near the Trevi Fountain, this attractive place takes food seriously while staying refreshingly inexpensive. Tried and true Roman specialties and fish specialties that follow the market's whims. Major credit cards.

Il Piccolo *(near Piazza Navona)* **$** *Via del Governo Vecchio 74; Tel. 06-68801746.* Open daily 11am–2am. Lively and casual, this is one of many popular wine bars popping up around town. This one also offers a buffet serving a limited selection of traditional fare in a characteristic neighborhood. Eat here before heading to the Piazza Navona for some street theater. Major credit cards.

Piperno *(Ghetto)* **$$$** *Via Monte dei Cenci 9, 00186; Tel. 06-68806629.* Lunch and dinner; closed Sunday for dinner and Monday. Opened in 1856, this longtime favorite in the heart of the Ghetto serves Roman/Jewish specialties, such as Jerusalem artichokes in a number of delicious variations. Reservations recommended. MC, V.

Pizzeria Baffetto *(near Piazza Navona)* **$** *Via del Governo Vecchio 114; Tel. 06-6861617.* Open daily, 6:30pm–1am; not open for lunch, closed Sunday November–February. A student hangout, beloved by all for the excellent pizza straight from the wood-burning oven. Despite a lengthy list, the plain and simple *margherita* is everyone's favorite. They can't make them fast enough. No credit cards.

Le Restaurant del Saint Regis Grand *(near Termini Station)* **$$$** *Via V.E. Orlando 3; Tel. 06-47091.* Lunch and dinner; closed Sunday. Sophisticated cuisine in the splendidly luxurious dining rooms of the Grand Hotel. The menu is international, but stick with the traditional Roman favorites, here perfectly prepared. A real treat if you're staying here; non-guests can make believe they are. Reservations essential. Major credit cards.

Romolo a Porta Settimiana *(Trastevere)* **$$** *Via di Porta Settimiana 8; Tel. 06-5818284; fax 06-5813043.* Lunch and dinner; closed Monday. Serving classic Roman cuisine and also some very creative pasta dishes, this place is well known for its outdoor dining in a charming garden, where one wall dates back 1,700 years. It's also delightful inside this upscale 400-year-old tavern. Reservations advised. Major credit cards.

La Rosetta *(Pantheon)* **$$$** *Via della Rosetta 9; Tel. 06-6861002; fax 06-68215116.* Lunch Thursday and Friday; dinner Monday–Saturday; closed Sunday. Considered the best seafood restaurant in Rome it has next to no meat options (carnivores, book elsewhere). Filet of sea bass with red wine sauce and artichokes is delicious. Imaginative use of spices and light sauces. Selection of international wines. Reservations essential. Major credit cards.

Sans Souci *(near Via Veneto)* **$$$** *Via Sicilia 20; Tel. 06-42014510.* Dinner only; closed Monday. For years one of Rome's most elegant restaurants offering a good range of international and traditional Roman dishes with a knowing emphasis on French cuisine. Old-time glamour and romance. Reservations recommended. Major credit cards.

Taverna Giulia *(Corso Vittorio Emanuele/Tiber)* **$$** *Vicolo dell'Oro 23; Tel. 06-6869768; fax 06-6893720.* Lunch and dinner; closed Sunday. An old favorite for enjoying the distinctive Ligurian cuisine — the most famous are the homemade pasta selections served with an excellent *pesto* (basil sauce). A favorite with visiting archbishops. Reservations recommended. Major credit cards.

T-Bone Station *(near Piazza di Spagna)* **$$** *Via F. Crispi; Tel. 06-6787650.* Lunch and dinner daily. For the homesick and the legions of Romans who love all things American, here are great steaks, hamburgers, French-fried onion rings, and brownies in an upbeat atmosphere. Major credit cards.

Trattoria della Pace *(near Piazza Navona)* **$$** *Via della Pace 1; Tel. 06-6864802.* Lunch and dinner; closed Monday. The dolce vita is back: If you want to see Hollywood stars at play, Bartolo Cuomo has created a stylish nest that features the cooking of his home-town, Amalfi. Tiny *pizzotelle* (baby puffy pizzas) and *scialatielli* (home-made short pasta from Amalfi with large shrimp) are favorites. Around the corner, his Bar della Pace promises serious people-watching. Reservations recommended, especially in the summer. DC, MC, V.

Trimani Wine Bar *(Piazza della Repubblica)* **$** *Via Cernaia 37/b; Tel. 06-4469661.* Lunch; dinner 5:30–12:30am; closed Sunday. An excellent choice of wines (the Trimani family first became famous for their nearby wine store) and good food is found in an elegant and friendly atmosphere. Sample a number of good-to-excellent wines by-the-glass accompanied by a light or full meal at very reasonable prices. Major credit cards.

Lazio

Adriano $$ *Via Villa Adriana, Tivoli; Tel. 0774-382235; fax 0774-535122.* Lunch and dinner; closed for dinner Sunday. Stop by here just outside the villa's gates for a plate of delicious home-made pasta, roast lamb, and a glass of wine after a walk around Hadrian's villa. Pleasant open-air dining in the summer. Major credit cards.

Allo Sbarco di Enea $$ *Via dei Romagnoli 675, 00119 Ostia Antica; Tel. and fax 06-5650034.* Lunch and dinner; closed Monday. Mock-ancient frescoes, chariots, and waiters decked out in Roman costumes. A convenient location between the station and the ruins. AE, MC, V.

Cecilia Metella *(Old Appian Way)* **$$** *Via Appia Antica 125/127, 00179; Tel. and fax 06-5136743.* Lunch and dinner; closed Monday. Pleasant, with an ample shady garden, near the Roman tomb of Cecilia Metella and especially popular for weddings, celebrations, and the traditional Sunday afternoon exodus when this area fills with Roman families. Major credit cards.

INDEX